W9-CIK-878

Dedication:

This book is dedicated to Scott Power. A true friend, an exceptional woodsman and the only person whom I can call and say, "remember when"? Thank you for sharing the adventure of a lifetime.

Special Thanks To:

My family, who let me follow my own footsteps. Dr. William Forgey, who made this adventure possible. Tracy Salcedo, for her diligent work on this book. The Stewart family, for allowing us into their home and cooking great meals for us year after year. Ernie, Robert and Manford for saving my life on the Churchill River. Randy Todd, for his "backcountry brewing wisdom". Nicole Villanueva, for understanding my dreams. And all of the people who told me I was crazy.

They have cradled you in custom,
they have primed you with their preaching,
They have soaked you in convention through and through;
They have put you in a showcase; you're a credit to their teaching-
But can't you hear the wild? - it's calling you.

Robert Service

Paradise Creek

A true story of adventure
in the Canadian wilderness

David Scott

Merrillville, IN

4700811

Paradise Creek

A true story of adventure in the Canadian wilderness.

Copyright © 1995 by David Scott
10 9 8 7 6 5 4 3 2 1

All rights reserved, including the right to reproduce this book or portions thereof in any form or by any means, electronic or mechanical, including photocopying and recording, unless authorization is obtained, in writing, from the publisher. Inquiries should be addressed to ICS BOOKS, 1370 East 86th Place, Merrillville, Indiana 46410.

Printed in U.S.A.

All ICS titles are printed on 50% recycled paper from pre-consumer waste. All sheets are processed without using acid.

Published by:
ICS BOOKS, Inc.
1370 E. 86th Place
Merrillville, IN 46410
800-541-7323

Co-Published by:
VANWELL PUBLISHING LTD.
1 Northrup Crescent
P.O. Box 2131,
St. Catharines, Ontario L2M 6P5.
800-661-6136

Library of Congress Cataloging-in-Publication Data

Scott, David. 1971-
    Paradise Creek: A true story of adventure in the Canadian wilderness /
    David Scott.
        p.   cm.
    ISBN 1-57034-009-9
    1. Frontier and pioneer life--Manitoba. 2. Scott, David. 1971-
    3. Adventure and adventurers--Manitoba--Biography.   4. Manitoba--
    Description and travel.   I. Title.
F1062.S36   1995
917. 12704 3 092--dc20
                                                                95-5310
                                                                CIP

Cover Photo: **Gerald Scott**
Inside Photos: **Scott Power and David Scott**

The Call

It was the 29th of January, 1991, and it was cold. Hap, our bush pilot, told us that the area was in the midst of a cold snap unlike any he'd seen in twenty years. The temperature at night dropped to 50° below zero and during the day it did not get much warmer. We were late departing that morning because it had to warm up to at least 40° below before he would fly.

Thoughts of the cold and the remoteness of the area flooded my mind as I listened to the drone of the engine. I watched, through the TV-like window of the plane, as mile after mile of frozen muskeg passed by. A few thousand feet down, the plane's shadow rippled over an endless carpet of black spruce trees. The deafening buzz of the engine faded to silence as I reflected on what Dr. Forgey once told me. "You know you're in the wilderness," he said, "when you can call for help and no one answers." I knew at last I was in such a place.

After an hour and a half, Hap banked the plane steeply to the right and pointed to a tiny dot nestled in the trees on the bank of the Little Beaver River. I swallowed deeply while staring at the cabin that was to be our home for the next 365 days.

Hap turned the plane and headed for a small lake

three miles from the cabin. We could have landed on the river, but that would have been all too easy. We wanted to plunge into the bone-chilling cold, and to embrace the arctic terrain. We wanted to toil in the infamous muskeg before claiming our pot of gold, so to speak, at the end of the rainbow.

The large yellow plane circled over Landing Lake patiently, like a giant falcon closing in on its prey, until finally our pilot eased the throttle back, extended the flaps and settled the bird gracefully upon the undisturbed snow.

It was one o'clock in the afternoon, Hap jumped out of the plane and sank to his pockets in the fine powdered snow. "I can only stay here a few minutes or she'll freeze up!" he said. Scott and I stared at each other for a second and then hastily began to move 1,500 pounds of gear from the plane's belly onto the wind-blown white drifts.

After a bit of hard work, we stood surrounded by several month's worth of provisions. Hap stood framed in the doorway of the plane with a rather perplexed look upon his brow. Scott and I smiled and waved a hearty goodbye; Hap rolled his eyes and wished us "Good luck," and slowly he closed the hatch. He was the last person we would see for months. The old yellow Otter taxied to the runway it had created only a few moments earlier, and with a roar, lifted off into the northern sky. The husky voice of the engine faded into the horizon and we heard for the first time the great silence of the North.

Finally, fantasy had become reality. The moment was at hand. Cold hung around our shoulders like a cloak, growing heavier with each passing second of our inactivity. It could not be seen, nor could it be heard. The cold was a force that could only be revered. Its presence was as fascinating as it was frightening.

But the silence . . . that subtle winter silence was even more intriguing, almost hypnotic. It seemed deafening to ears so accustomed to sound, and it became, to me, more mysterious and more powerful than the cold.

Together, the silence and the cold shrouded the black spruce forest, and my partner and I stood alone in the midst of our great adventure.

"It's just going to be a short three hour hike from the lake to the cabin," I thought as I strapped on my snow shoes. The plane had covered the distance in less than a minute. We put on our packs, checked the map, and headed into the woods on a 291º bearing. It didn't take more than a few steps before we realized this was not going to be a short hike. The trees grow extremely close together in this country, their limbs were locked and entangled, making walking difficult and navigation nearly impossible. In this dense, flat terrain there are few landmarks, so we had to check and re-check the compass bearing every few steps. To make matters worse, in extreme low temperatures snow takes on the characteristics of fine powdered sugar. Rather than walking upon it, you wade through it, carrying the snow that piles on top of your snowshoes with every step.

After an hour of hiking all I could think was that in two hours we would be at the cabin. We'd have a warm fire, a hot cup of coffee and dinner . . . those thoughts kept my feet moving and my level of excitement high.

Three hours later, we were still walking. The temperatures continued to drop as darkness fell upon us. No river and no cabin. We hiked on through the dense woods, aided by the light of a full moon. Were it not for the lunar light, darkness would have forbidden our travel, forcing us to camp in the ice-bitten forest. We continued to check our heading as we walked until finally, we saw it. The silvery vein of the river shining in the light of the pale moon.

"There it is," I heard my partner say, "the river!"

With new-found energy, we plunged down the gradual slope that led to our new wilderness home. I thought, "It won't be long now," and then I remembered what Doc had told us. "The cabin is a three-hour hike from Landing Lake. When you see the river, you're halfway there."

"Halfway there!" I thought. "We've already been hiking for more than four hours, we should be there by now. Surely we are more than halfway."

Doc was right of course. We continued to hike for another three hours before finally arriving on the river bank. The jagged fangs of the black spruce trees sank themselves deeply into the face of the moon, and every now and then the winter night would take a deep breath, causing the snow from the tree limbs to fall silently to the ground. Seven hours had gone by since we'd stepped from the plane. We were hungry, exhausted and nearly hypothermic. We hadn't eaten in 12 hours. Our bodies had no fuel from which to generate heat. We now had only one thought . . . find the cabin!

We broke a snowshoe trail down the river for a quarter mile or so, every now and then zig-zagging into the woods, searching for the cabin. We knew that it was no more than thirty yards from the river bank, yet as hard and as desperately as we looked, we found nothing but a dense pristine wilderness.

It didn't add up. Everywhere we looked, there was beauty, but we felt like we were in hell. As we turned to hike back along the trail we'd just broken we saw that it shone like a neon ribbon in the snow on the river. The black trees, dappled with downy flakes of white snow, the white snow painted with long black shadows, the ample moon, the brilliant stars, the absolute stillness . . . the beauty was breathtaking. Yet this beauty was equally deceiving, for it was beginning to absorb the heat and the life from our bodies.

We were in trouble, and we were well aware of that fact. Thinking perhaps the cabin was in the other direction, we searched up river for two hours with no luck. Our situation was desperate. We didn't bring a tent, for we'd assumed the hike would be completed quickly. We had just learned the first rule of the North: Never make assumptions when your life is at stake. Our options narrowed to one, make a shelter fast and attempt to stay alive until dawn.

The extreme cold had drawn the suppleness from even the largest spruce boughs. They snapped easily and our A-frame shelter went up in less than half an hour. We tried to pile snow on top of the hastily built structure for insulation, but it would simply sift down through the lattice work of spruce needles. Like bears digging out a den, we scraped snow from inside the shelter. We then laid pine boughs and sleeping pads on the floor for extra insulation. By this time, the cold was slowly sinking through our several layers of clothing, and into our flesh. We felt groggy and disoriented. Scott opened one of our sleeping bags and laid it flat on the floor. We both climbed into the other bag, pulled the open one around us, and hugged each other to share what little heat we had. Once settled inside, we prepared ourselves for the longest, the coldest, and perhaps the final night of our lives.

I'm not sure when I first heard "the call," but as far back as I can remember, I've had a passion for nature and an insatiable lust for adventure. By the time I was eight years old, I'd driven a dog team to the North pole, climbed to the top of Mt. Everest, and hunted buffalo with the Indians. These adventures all happened in a small woods near my home in northwest Indiana, within the magical reality of my imagination.

My real adventure began the day I found an arrowhead in a farmer's field near the woods. I became fascinated with this rare race of people who had lived a life that I'd only read about. They had a relationship with nature that I wanted to experience.

I wanted more than imagination, more than make-believe, I wanted the real thing . . . I wanted adventure.

Over the next ten years, I spent time living in the backcountry of Wyoming's Teton mountains, hiking through Isle Royale in Lake Superior, and canoeing through parts of northern Minnesota. Although these were great adventures, they still did not dowse the fire that burned within me. I wanted more, I wanted to step back in time and live like a pioneer.

One day, while working for a local outfitter, I met the person who would help make my dream become a reality, Dr. William Forgey, physician, author, adventurer and international authority on wilderness medicine. Because we both thrived on the legend and lore of the North Country, we became instant friends. Through discussion, I learned that while I was dreaming, Forgey was doing. Near the time I was born he'd built a small log cabin in the vast untamed wilderness of northern Canada. I was, of course, interested in everything he had to say about this cabin and its surrounding country. Sensing my interest he said, "We'll have to see if we can get you up there, kid."

I was sure it was nothing more than a passing remark until the phone rang one week later.

"Dave, how does one year at the cabin sound to you . . . think you'd be interested?" It was Scott Power, a friend of Doc's and a recent acquaintance of mine. At the time he was twenty years old, one year older than myself. "Sure," I said, rather flattered, but still never believing it would actually happen.

"Why don't we get together and begin planning it out," Scott said, in what I would come to find as his usual enthusiastic manner.

For the next several months, we put every thought, plan, and idea down on paper. We checked and re-checked our lists. We compared our lists to the lists of others who had previously been at the cabin, and we started purchasing gear. Due to the remoteness of the cabin, Doc trained us extensively in wilderness first aid, providing us also with a sense of self-confidence in case an accident were to take place. Even during all this preparation, I still didn't believe it would ever happen. The adventure that was once a dream still seemed like some far-away fantasy. We fine-tuned every last detail, made all the last-minute arrangements and before I knew it, we were flying in a 1956 DeHavilland Otter above the endless wilds of the vast Canadian wilderness.

Now however, the intense heat of adrenaline I had felt only twelve hours earlier was replaced by the cold sweat of fear. Now the adventure was more alive, and more real than I would have liked it to be. It was no longer a dream but a nightmare that was slowly taking the life away from myself and my friend.

Every fifteen or twenty minutes, one would shake the other and ask, "You OK?" The response was generally a chattered stuttering. "Yeah, yeah, I'm OK." We assured one another that everything would be all right, regardless of the fact that the temperature was 63° below zero. Eventually, we began mumbling and promising that someone would come and take us home.

But no one came, and in the depths of the forest, nothing stirred. So it went for the next eight or ten hours, my odyssey of the North and the beginning of a childhood dream.

Back home in the states, our family and friends were going to bed feeling rather certain that we'd made it to the cabin. If they only knew.

The night did not pass easily into morning. Finally, we saw the light of a new day shining between the lacy branches of our shelter. I raised my head through a powdery veil of snow and wondered for a brief moment whether I was dead or alive. The roof of our tiny shelter, as well as our sleeping bag, was covered with a shell of frost and ice from our breath. Outside, our packs sat half buried in the snow, and each was coated with a thick crust of ice. Both packs were full of food, yet it all required cooking and shelter was our top priority. The sun was mentally motivational, but nonetheless, we were cold, intensely cold. We hadn't eaten in 24 hours and we hadn't found the cabin. With each passing moment, our situation worsened. However, on the positive side, we were alive. We rose and struggled to step into our frozen mukluks.

"I'll look upstream and you look downstream. If we don't find the cabin in a couple of hours, we'll have to go back to Landing Lake and re-group," I told Scott.

We both set off, cutting into the woods at frequent intervals to get a closer look at anything we thought might resemble a cabin. Two hours later, we met back at the bivouac site. Nothing needed to be said. We could tell by the look on the other's face that the cabin had not been found. Scott and I both howled curses into the clear blue sky. The wilds ignored our insults, and the fine powdered snow engulfed our echoing shouts. "Yell your head off for help and no one will hear you." Doc's haunting words echoed in my mind. We were without question in such a place. Where was the cabin? What had gone wrong?

Disappointed, we headed back along the trail we'd broken the day before. At this point, sheer anger was our only source of heat. The semi-packed snow knocked five hours off the return trip, two hours later we were back where we had started. A moose had ambled over our trail the night before, leaving hip-deep footprints in the snow and making the final one hundred yards of travel one hundred yards of hell. If only our bodies were as well equipped for the conditions as his!

We hastily rummaged through our duffels and found the canvas expedition tent that was Doc's pride and joy. It came complete with a stove and stove-pipe. We set it up on the spot. Yet, of course, there was a slight problem. One piece of stove-pipe was missing. Doc had informed us before our departure that the missing piece was at the cabin. We had brought the tent and stove along to use on expeditions after we reached the cabin; we'd never worried about this tiny detail, for we honestly didn't believe we'd sleep in the tent before sleeping in the cabin.

The old sourdoughs or "gold scrapers" had a name for people such as Scott and myself: "Cheechako." Cheechako simply means "greenhorn." Although our knowledge of the outdoors was rather extensive, we began to understand that this Northern-most University was not interested in such things as knowledge. What it wanted was wisdom. If one had no experience, he learned quickly and rather painfully on a lonely trail, or he was left as food for the barren land. If he was fortunate enough to make it out of the North Country alive, he most likely departed with an incomplete set of fingers or toes. Hindsight has given me this perspective, but at the time, all we knew was that we had to get warm, and that was all there was to it.

We fashioned the missing section of pipe with a piece of tin foil. Not the safest rig, but in a pinch (and we were in a pinch) it would have to do. We filled the tank with kerosene, and moments later the stove popped and sputtered into action. At last, we were going to be warm. We filled a pot with snow for water, and set it on the stove.

"What'll it be?" my partner hollered as he rummaged through one of the food duffels. "Beef in a bag, sweet & sour shrimp, or spaghetti with meat balls?"

"All three," I replied, too exhausted to move.

Within minutes, the snow in the pot began to melt and waves of heat filled the tent. At last we were going to exercise a bit of control over our situation. Breathing a sigh of relief, I settled back to relax, when suddenly my partner yelled "FIRE!" (along with a colorful array of invectives). I took my eyes off the only water in liquid form above ground for one hundred and twenty miles to see that the top of our tent was on fire. Damn it! What in the hell was going on? It seemed as though our makeshift stove-pipe section couldn't cut it. No sooner had the tent caught fire than flames began popping from the bottom of the stove itself. With his big down mitts, Scott violently whacked at the stove, and sent it flying out the door. After that, we both stood and clapped the smoldering canvas with our mitts. After a few minutes the danger had passed and a lonely gray sky peered down upon us through a huge black eye in the roof of our tattered tent. Outside, the stove hissed in a melting ring of snow. Scott and I looked at each other, and then down at the water in the pot that was to have been part of our dinner. During the brief period of hysteria, it had frozen solid. Though we had another tent, we were too cold and tired to set it up--besides it was beginning to get dark. I grabbed a half dozen granola bars and a few squares of frozen fudge, climbed into my sleeping bag, and impatiently sucked on the munchies until they thawed enough to swallow.

Somehow, the events of the last twenty-four hours didn't live up to the romantic Jack London vision I'd created in my mind. "It's funny," I thought, "how the slightest mistake in an unforgiving place such as this can turn into an uncontrollable disaster." Fortunately, our annoying disasters hadn't been fatal, at least thus far.

I went to sleep with the incredible events on my mind. I thought about Murphy's law: What can go wrong, will go wrong. It certainly applied in our case.

That night, the infamous North taught us yet another lesson. Never set up camp in the open. Of course, we were already well aware of this "golden rule," yet, because we were cold and exhausted, we set the tent up right where we had found it, (living up to our Cheechako reputation). We had no sooner gotten to sleep when a violent storm whipped up and almost blew us off the lake. Even though our tent was close to the protection of the bank, it didn't seem to make a difference. The winds ripped and lashed at the canvas until I thought it would be torn to shreds. Mercifully, the storm lasted only a couple of hours, and by morning all was calm.

Breakfast was a mouthful of frozen fudge, and we each took a handful of hard candy for the trail, not quite eggs benedict with a side of toast and a spot of tea, but it would have to suffice. We hastily packed each sled with about seventy five pounds of gear, and once again we were on our way.

Our bodies were fatigued and our minds were boggled. The sheer will to live seemed to be the only fuel for our tired legs. As for actual energy obtained from food and drink, we'd had next to none.

With every step, I thought about where the cabin might be. Scott had been there once for a short summer visit about two years earlier. He knew that it was about thirty yards from the bank, on a long graceful bend in the river. I knew the heading of 291º from Landing Lake was correct. The cabin should be within a few yards of our bivouac site, which was also on a graceful bend in the river. Nothing made sense. We wandered in circles trying to find the structure, attempting to figure out what the problem was. Then, frustrated, we gave up, went back to the river just past noon and began to set up camp.

This time we set up a more modern geodesic dome-style tent built by Eureka, but as we were setting it up, we received yet another surprise. Under normal conditions, a tent like this can go up in five minutes or less. But this was a country where mercury can be frozen solid and used as a paper weight for a great part of the year. These were far from normal conditions. In such cold temperatures, the shock cord that holds the pole sections together loses all of its elasticity. It expands but will not contract. Before the poles could be fitted together, 56 shock cord sections had to be cut one by one and we had to remove our gloves in order to do so. It sounds easy enough, but at 50° below, with frozen, stiff, and shaking fingers, it was a giant test of will. Once the cords were cut, the poles were carefully fed through nylon sleeves. A curtain of darkness was slowly descending upon our forest stage, and descending with it was the temperature. After thirty-five minutes, the tent was up. I vividly recall looking at Scott and being frightened. His face was discolored, and his eyelids were nearly welded shut with a thick bead of ice. His body shook uncontrollably, and his speech was becoming slurred.

The tent could not have been set a moment later than it was. The cold was intensely painful, preventing us from efficiently completing even the most minor task. We had to watch our fingers in order to use them, for nothing could be accomplished merely by sense of touch. With great difficulty, the stove was lit. At that point we did not care about asphyxiation, we did not care if we burned the tent to the ground. We would be warm, and that was all we cared about. Fortunately, neither of the two had happened. For the first time since our landing, we were able to remove some of our outer gear and experience the caressing hands of warmth.

After the feeling returned to our fingertips and the blood began to thaw and flow more freely through our veins, we started melting snow for food and drink. When we opened the door of our tent to retrieve more snow, the cold air from outside would clash with the warm air inside and form a huge billow of steam. The cold was intense, and our luck was incredible. How we ever managed to stay alive in those conditions, with such little fuel in our bodies, was beyond me. But we were still without a cabin, so the game wasn't over yet.

The third night descended upon us quietly, bringing with it the cold. The sight of our bivouac nestled in the snow humbled our conversation and reminded us how deceiving that beauty could be. Scott and I each devoured a four-man freeze-dried meal and drank nearly one gallon of water apiece. All of the spoons were at the cabin, so we shared the flat battery cover from a small flashlight we'd brought along.

After dinner, we carpeted the tent floor with maps and began poring over topographic details by flickering candlelight. The trusty stove continued to sputter away, warming our tiny Nylon bubble, when suddenly, without warning, it faded and died. Neither Scott nor I even considered the obvious possibility that the stove could be out of fuel; our immediate reaction was "more bad luck." Instantly, the temperature in the tent was 40° below zero, leaving us, once again, prey to the merciless cold. Our teeth chattered and our fingers grew stiff. I quickly re-fueled the stove, primed it and moments later it was sputtering away again.

To prime the stove, we had to dump about half an ounce of fuel on the burner, ignite the fuel and then turn on the stove valve. The result is very much like that of a flambé meal served at a fancy restaurant. Technically speaking, such a flame has no place inside a four-man nylon tent. This practice is greatly frowned upon by most campers, but when warmth is a matter of life and death, even the most law-abiding camper would say, "the hell with it," and burn the rule book.

Once warm, Scott and I tried to figure out just where we were. Logic may have told us differently, but instinct made us believe we were downstream from the cabin. Tomorrow, we would travel upstream, and by nightfall, not only be warm, but also have some stretching room in our home-to-be. Things were finally beginning to brighten a bit in the warmth of the tent (they couldn't have gotten much worse). However, in the back of my mind, I knew that Mother Nature would waste no time in thwarting that optimism. In looking at the map, the river appeared to be incredibly vast and the cabin was just a mere dot upon its shore.

Scott and I both burrowed deep within our bags before shutting down the stove. Outside, the wind picked up and composed eerie songs through the jagged spruce tops. Our tent shuddered on the bank of the river, a tiny womb in which lay two very uncertain souls. Yet, one thing was for certain, we were alive!

I remember awakening in the middle of the night having to answer nature's call in a rather serious way. Of course I encountered a slight problem (beside the fact that I had to climb from my warm bag in forty-below temperatures). I discovered that the zipper on our tent was welded shut with a thick bead of ice. No matter how hard I tried, it wouldn't budge. Not only was I shaking violently from the cold, but I had to GO! Finally, I held a lighter (which I kept in my sleeping bag to prevent it from freezing) near the ice to melt it. After nearly dying of hypothermia, I got some relief!

The sun was soon beaming through the slate-gray tent roof. I know I slept well that night, for Scott was awake and making coffee before I even thought of opening my eyes. "Well, today's the day!" I remember my partner saying when I finally awakened.

Neither of us were in any great hurry. Sure, the

thought of finding the cabin was more than exciting, yet it also meant becoming cold once again, and warmth was something we had just rediscovered.

Scott was in the process of taking off his socks to change into warmer clothing when I heard him curse under his breath.

"What's the matter?" I asked.

Scott slowly lifted his foot from behind his sleeping bag; the expression on his face said it all. His heel, his toes, and the ball of his right foot was as swollen and black as a northern night. I stared in disbelief, not knowing what to say.

For a great while, Scott held his foot in the air and shook his head back and forth. This couldn't possibly be happening. We'd planned too long and come too far to encounter such a calamity. But there it was, a symbol of our struggle.

I was, of course, concerned about Scott's foot, but even more, I was concerned about Scott himself. I began to wonder how he would respond to his condition given our present circumstances. One word kept creeping into my mind . . . panic. We had to keep our cool, and we had to keep our sense of focus. After all, we still had a cabin to find.

Although I didn't know what to say to cushion the blow, I did know what to do. Before we left for the cabin, Doc had prepared Scott and me for a broad spectrum of medical emergencies. Frostbite was obviously one of them, and I instantly flashed back to the day he explained frostbite treatment to us. (As I recall it was nearly 80 degrees outside.)

First, Doc instructed, the frozen part should be thawed in warm water (approximately 110º). This is a painful process that normally takes 25 to 30 minutes. The frostbitten part should thaw until its color becomes pink or burgundy red, but no longer. However, Doc also had said this should not be done if there was any risk of refreezing. Refreezing a frostbitten and thawed part could result in substantial tissue loss, gangrene or auto-amputation.

Ultimately, what this meant was that our two-man team was now a one-man team. I had so desperately wanted to look for the cabin that morning, yet I knew that I would have to head back to Landing Lake for the medical kit and more supplies. I was concerned, Scott was angry, and we still did not have a cabin.

The trip back to the lake went quickly. As I snowshoed up the trail, I thought of our night in the bivouac. Virtually all night long, I had complained about the excruciating pain in my feet. Scott, on the other hand, had said his feet didn't hurt at all . . . obviously they were frozen. To quote an old expression of the North, they were "bit to the bone" the first night out. Because of the burning pain, I had massaged my bare feet between my hands. Had I not, they would have looked identical to Scott's. From that point on I vowed never to say "it can't get any worse," because it could, and if you didn't believe it, it would.

Our giant canvas tent was beaten down flush with the snow on the lake. After a few minutes of fumbling around, I found the door and snaked my way inside. I grabbed the medical kit, some munchies, and a few more candles. Out of curiosity, I opened Doc's book, *Wilderness Medicine*, to the section on frostbite. The first thing I read was this:

"... Peter Freuchen, the great Greenland explorer, once walked days and miles keeping his leg frozen, knowing that when the leg thawed, he would be helpless. He lost his leg, but saved his life!"

"Great," I thought, "I can't let Scott read that, who knows what he'll do."

I continued to pack the long army duffel with provisions. Then, I walked over to where our 1,500 pounds of gear was buried beneath a snow drift. I rummaged through some of the duffels in hopes of finding anything that might prove useful. I found several packages of freeze-dried food and also our five gallons of white gas. The sun was beginning to set, as I loaded everything on my sled and once again headed for the river.

With darkness falling about me some new fears, other than the cold, began to work in my mind. Churchill, aside from having a population of only 750 people, is known as the polar bear capital of the world. Even though we were 125 miles away, the thought of being the only easily obtainable fresh meat in the vicinity was not a comforting one. One of the groups that had visited the cabin in the past had seen a polar bear across the river from the cabin. Because the chances of my seeing a great white bear were slim, I put the thought out of my mind and kept snowshoeing along, weaving my sled through the black, gnarled tree trunks.

The predicament of Scott's toes became rather minute, dwarfed by the vastness of the dark frozen swamp. I tried to whistle a tune but my lips were too cracked to carry a melody. I tried to sing but my breath was too short from the work. Finally, I settled for just making a lot of noise, and I thought as I hiked along that my idea would do one of two things. Either it would scare the "big bad wolves" away, or it would let them know where I was. I took my chances!

In my hands I clutched an old Marlin .30-.30, and in the pale moonlight, I could see its silver barrel swinging back and forth in time with my unbalanced steps. Attempting to knock down an angry polar bear with such a weapon would be like trying to drop a bowling pin with a marble. At best it would only upset such a powerful creature, but it did provide a false sense of security. I must admit that the thought of a hungry bear made my feet shuffle a bit faster.

I was relieved when I saw the tent through the trees. The tiny dome was illuminated with the flickering light from a candle. My snowshoes crunched through the powdery snow, and when I heard Scott call out my name, I quickly responded. It's funny how concerned we became about each other while in the bush. When separated, Scott and I constantly thought about each other's welfare, for we were now dependent upon each other.

I quickly dove into the tent, ripped off my down mitts and warmed my hands over the stove. Scott had his foot slightly elevated, with cotton gauze bandages loosely wrapped and tucked between each toe. Surprisingly enough, some of the color had returned to his heel and the ball of his foot, yet we were still concerned about his toes.

Scott prepared freeze-dried beef stroganoff for dinner. Meanwhile, I handed Scott the antibiotics Doc had prescribed to ward off infection. When he saw Doc's book *Wilderness Medicine* sticking out of my pocket, he said, "Read me the section on frostbite."

Needless to say, I edited the part about Peter Freuchen losing his leg.

Later, we looked over the maps, searching for any hint that might help us in our quest. Again, we decided that I should search upstream.

I slid into my bag feeling certain I'd find the cabin in the morning. Scott was putting the maps back into his day pack when he came across the letter Doc had given us the day we left. With the letter, Doc had also given us specific instructions not to open it until the third night out (we were a day late) it read:

Well, you guys are finally at the cabin. I just want you to know how proud I am of you. Do me a favor, walk down to the bank of the river and think about me. You know I'll be thinking of you. Don't forget the motto of the North West Co. "Persevere". Best wishes and good luck.

Friends always,
Doc

Our first impression was to laugh at the irony of the entire scenario. If only he knew where we were. Yet we realized this was far from a laughing matter, for God's sake, we had no cabin. When the last drop of fuel was burned from our stove, we would more than likely perish, the snow would cover us, and the rhythm of this place would go on as if nothing had happened.

With that in mind, we didn't talk of the cabin, we didn't even say good night, we simply turned off the stove, blew out the candle, and went to sleep. Outside the wind howled, and Doc's voice echoed in my mind.

". . . And no one will hear you."

I didn't sleep well that night, whether because of nervousness or cold I do not know. I felt confident my journey upstream tomorrow would prove profitable, but what if it wasn't? I laid for a long time with my eyes wide open, staring through the tiny blow-hole of my sleeping bag at the roof of the tent. I could not see the steam from my breath rise, but I could feel it fall back upon my lips in a misty spray. We had learned quickly never to breath inside our bags. Doing so caused the bag to become soggy and eventually it turned into a synthetic ice cube.

Morning came slowly. First, the sky was a slate gray, then a dull blue, and finally a brilliant white. I laid awake in my bag procrastinating the cold process of lighting the stove. Finally, with no other alternative, I counted down 3 . . . 2 . . . 1 and jumped out to face the chilling embrace of the North. I pumped the tiny stove as fast as I could to pressurize the fuel tank. Then, I poured a half ounce of fuel on the burner pan and touched it with a lighted wooden match, causing it to jolt to life with an audible poof.

Doc had cautioned us about using fuel in subzero temperatures, saying that it becomes much like liquid nitrogen. Spilling fuel on exposed flesh would cause instant frostbite, something we had more than our share of. Even the aluminum fuel bottle had to be handled with gloved hands.

Within seconds, our small dome tent began to

thaw. Walls that were sagging now drew taut from the heat, much like a hot-air balloon. Ice build-up on the tent roof, caused by our breath, melted and slid down to the tent floor. I wrestled with the frozen zipper to open the door, greet the morning and grab some snow. The weather was beautiful, freezing cold, but beautiful. Ten feet from our tent sat the bivouac, and I knew we could have still been within its wooden tomb. I filled the pots with snow and tunneled my way back inside, ignoring the thought.

The first item on the menu was, of course, coffee. Very, very, very black coffee. Scott climbed out of his sleeping bag, enticed by the smell of the rich concoction.

We ate freeze-dried spaghetti using a battery cover for a spoon, drank several cups of coffee, and talked about everything except the cabin, for fear we would somehow be jinxed. After breakfast, I put on my outer gear, and prepared myself mentally for the search.

"Good luck." I heard Scott call from the tent.

After stepping outside and lacing up my snowshoes, he called again. I peered into the tent while shivering and attempting to stay warm.

"Be careful, O.K." Again, I gave him a thumbs-up and headed up the frozen river, which wove through the land like a giant white vein upon an old gnarled hand.

Several thoughts passed lazily through my mind as I trudged along. I remembered how people had responded when I told them what I was about to do.

"Well, is this some sort of school project ? . . Are you conducting a scientific experiment ? . . Are you doing some research ? . . Will you receive credits for this 'vacation' ? . . WHY?"

The last was a question that I had long since become accustomed to, but had never had a solid answer for. The trip wasn't in the name of science, nor was it to be "the first." We weren't going because "it was there," nor were we going to receive college credits. When I told people that our reason was simply for the experience, most of their enthusiasm turned into criticism.

"You're gonna get yourself killed . . . Why are you spending your time so foolishly? . . When will you get on with your life? . . Do you ever plan on going to school? . . Don't you have a job?"

"Funny," I thought to myself as I hiked along, "One block off the well-worn path, and *voila* we're crazy." It seemed an appropriate label, since we weren't pursuing the proverbial American dream (and, of course, everybody needs a label). People thought Lindbergh was insane, and Edison was foolish; they thought the Wright brothers were wasting their time, and they thought Thoreau was a twinkie or two short of a picnic. The world wants nothing more than for a man to conform to its traditions, yet, at the same time, the world comes to worship those who have broken free of convention and conformity. Those men and many others like them weren't crazy at all; they were pioneers. The way I saw it, if the majority of people thought my experience in the North was foolish and crazy, I knew it was the right thing to do!

Sure, I had some people tell me how they'd just love to go up there for a "vacation". I still don't know if they really meant what they said or if they had any concept of what this adventure entailed. Scott and I understood that to maintain sanity for a prolonged period of time in the bush, we had to do a great deal more than enjoy our surroundings. This trip required work, physically, mentally and spiritually.

Onward through the snow I trudged. The snow on the river was a little crusty on top, allowing me to move along its surface with a little more ease. Again, I zig-zagged from the river to the woods searching for any clue that might lead me to the cabin. My body began to stiffen as the cold tightened its grip, and still I saw nothing that resembled a cabin, or even a good location for one. My legs were growing tired, and because of the steam building up on my lenses, my sunglasses became useless.

After walking a mile or so, I was beginning to get discouraged. Then I noticed the mouth of a stream that fed the Little Beaver River, a stream that we would later call Paradise Creek. I plodded along, studying the banks on either side. The east bank appeared to be the perfect site for a cabin, but Doc had mentioned his cabin was on the upstream side of a feeder stream. The west bank (the upstream bank) was very low, far too low for a cabin. I was puzzled.

I passed beneath some of the largest spruce trees I had seen since the trip began, which gave me a rather bizarre idea.

Removing my snowshoes, I began to work my way up through the tangled limbs of the largest tree I could find. I must have looked pretty foolish in the eyes of other animals, attempting such a climb in full winter garb. However, after many twists, turns and scratches, I reached the top.

With a bird's eye view, I slowly panned the surrounding area. Again, I saw nothing that resembled a man-made structure, but I did see a lake. A very small one, but a lake nonetheless. From my lofty perch, it stuck out like a sore thumb. Doc had never mentioned anything about a lake. I thought to myself, "Where in the hell am I?" I slid out on a limb and strained my eyes to take in every detail of the area, and once again I saw no sign of the cabin or even a good location for one.

Discouraged, I carefully maneuvered myself down the tree, knowing that if I were to fall the game would be over. The sun was beginning to merge with the jagged tree tops by the time I reached the ground. Quickly, I strapped on my snowshoes and headed back down the trail I'd broken earlier. I had not found the cabin, but I had found some clues that would perhaps take me to its door.

Tomorrow, I was going to find it. Enough was enough!

Darkness fell quickly, as I crunched my way toward the illuminated bubble that sat nestled in the snow.

"Scott!" I shouted.

"Did ya find it?" he replied.

I took off my snowshoes and dove into the tent to warm my aching fingers.

"No," I replied as I opened the maps.

"Well, it looks like you found something," he said hopefully.

"It's just a hunch," I said. "Can you light another candle?"

Scott busied himself with the candle while I squinted at the wrinkled map. My finger traced the pale blue line of the river. Near a bend I found the feeder stream. Its eastern bank was slightly elevated, its western bank was flat; and set back in the woods to the southwest was a tiny lake. For the first time I had a clue as to where we were. Doc's cabin sat on a graceful bend in the river. One mile upstream from his cabin was an identical bend, the bend on which we were camped.

I explained my theory to Scott and we both agreed that the cabin had to be downstream. We were willing to bet our lives on it!

Excitement filled the tent that night. Scott made some freeze-dried sweet-and-sour shrimp for dinner and we celebrated with vanilla pudding for dessert. We kept on pointing at the map and laughing at our ignorance. Yet, we wondered why on earth had we punched out of the woods one mile upstream? Well, that didn't matter now, we felt certain that within 24 hours we would find our new home.

Before bedding down, I dug into the medical kit to retrieve more gauze for Scott's foot. It was showing some signs of improvement; in fact, all of the blackness had faded with the exception of his big toe, which remained as black as a lump of coal. I must say I was amazed at the way he handled his predicament. He didn't panic in the least. I wonder to this day what I would have done had my foot been bitten.

Sleep, of course, was next to impossible. I didn't want to get my hopes too high, but there was no stopping them now. I remembered feeling this way the night before we flew into the bush, excited, anxious and scared. But now . . . now, after being taunted and tortured for one week, we were finally near our mark. The dream that had captivated me as a child could be one mile away from becoming reality; it was a possibility well worth hoping for.

When I awakened, the sun was an hour old. I didn't hesitate to get out of my bag and face the cold, for the sooner I bellied my breakfast, the sooner I would be on the trail. Within minutes, the stove was roaring, the coffee was boiling, the tent was thawing, and our spirits were soaring. Scott rolled out of his bag with a big smile stretching across his face.

Beef stroganoff and strong coffee was the morning meal, which I shoveled down rapidly. After breakfast, I spread out the maps for one last look. Neither of us mentioned finding the cabin. "In one hour, this is where I will be," I said with confidence pointing at the map. Quickly, I wrapped myself in down gear and before long the tent looked like a tiny dot on the river bank.

For some reason, it didn't seem nearly as cold as it had during the past five days, which made travel, even through the deep snow, a bit more tolerable. But I hadn't walked more than a half mile downstream when those notorious "what ifs" started popping into my head. What if the cabin isn't there? What if I fall through the ice? What if the roof of the cabin is caved in? What if, what if, what if? I tried to put everything into the closet of my mind, and focus simply on walking.

According to the map, the river below our bivouac made a slow bend to the east, and then rolled into a long wide straight-away, followed by another bend to the northwest. Slowly, I waded through the powdery snow. Reaching the first bend seemed to take forever, yet soon I found myself standing in the middle of a river runway, long, straight and wide. From a distance, it appeared the river made a turn toward the northwest as the map indicated, yet I still wasn't certain.

Distances, as we had learned our first night out, could be quite deceiving in this flat snow-covered, terrain. I believed it would take me 30 minutes at the most to hike the straight section, but it actually seemed as though I was on a snow-covered treadmill. Onward I trudged, allowing my hopes and excitement to mount with every step.

Soon, I could see that the river did indeed bend to the northwest. If my calculations were correct, the cabin would be between me and that bend. Further ahead, on the eastern bank, I could see a feeder stream. I remembered how Doc once described the cabin as being the proverbial oasis in the desert. Hell, I didn't necessarily need a pot of gold at the end of the rainbow; a nice hot cup of java in a cabin at the end of the trail would suit me just fine. I heard the wind slowly breathe through the stunted spruce trees, like a haunting symphony composed in an empty orchestra hall. Between each wind song, the only sound was that of my snowshoes crunching through the crystals of powdery snow. Then, I stopped. Looking to the east I saw an open space amidst a solid wall of spruce trees. The opening worked up a tiny hill, and appeared rather un-natural in comparison to the rest of the landscape. With my snowshoes, I stamped a large "X" in the trail so that I could investigate this spot on my return trip. Taking one more step, but not taking my eyes off that gap, I saw a mound of snow that rose fifteen feet above the ground.

Slowly, I walked into the trees toward the mound, trying not to be overly optimistic. I held my breath and the sound of the snow crunching beneath my snowshoes grew louder with every step. Three steps into the trees, I collapsed in the waist deep-snow. Tears ran down my face and froze upon my wind-burned and chapped cheeks. There before me, cloaked in a royal robe of white, sat the cabin, patiently awaiting my arrival. I was paralyzed with euphoria, and for the better part of five minutes, all I could do was sit in the snow and stare.

My childhood dream now sat before me like a gem upon the downy flakes of fresh snow. I rose to my feet and deliberately stepped toward the weathered walls, removing my gloves to touch them. Indeed . . . they were real! I strolled around the structure and removed the shutters from the three small windows. I found the door around back. The handle was a piece of thick leather from the shoulder strap of a Duluth pack. It was locked with a crowbar, just as Doc had said it would be. With a little effort, I removed the bar and kicked open the door, which had been frozen shut. My gun-barrel entered the cabin first. The way our luck had been going, I'd probably walk right into a hibernating she-bear (most likely with cubs). Fortunately, all was silent and still. Squinting in the dim light, I saw four kerosene lamps hanging from a wooden peg that was driven into one of the wall logs. Two of the four had a little fuel left in their tanks, and, after a few minutes, I managed to ignite one of them. The kerosene flame illuminated the tiny room with a dull but adequate light.

The cabin itself consisted of three separate rooms. The main room was twelve by twelve by six, with a loft that was four-and-a-half feet tall at its highest point. Adjoining the cabin to the north was a tool shed that was twelve feet long and four feet wide. Its roof sloped from the main cabin to the ground. To the south was a room appropriately called the south wing. It also was twelve feet long, and four feet wide, but its roof did not slope to the ground; three four-foot walls allowed more storage room. The south wing, which happened to be where I was standing, was the entryway to the cabin.

Slowly, my eyes adjusted to the dim lighting and panned the tiny room. Each corner was packed with bits and pieces of dried grass, pine needles, and what ever else the resident animals could gather for warm nests. The floor was strewn with martin scat, and every item on the supply shelves was overturned. The cabin was trashed, but I was not about to complain. There was, I noticed, one item on the supply shelves that remained undisturbed, a one-liter bottle of vodka. I'm not certain if I did it for festive reasons, or merely for the hell of it, but I spun the cap off and had a hearty belt. I could feel the liquor burn a path straight to my boots. Of course, I foolishly forgot that the alcohol was nearly super cooled, so after my slug I had to wipe away the tears brought about by the liquor.

Grabbing my lantern I opened the door, that led into the main cabin, and squeezed inside.

The sun cut thin streams of light through the frosted windows; everything was perfectly silent and still. Like the south wing, the main cabin was a mess, yet on the positive side, the roof was attached, the walls were intact, and the stove appeared functional. Duffels hung heavy with supplies from nails in the rafters, and two empty chairs sagged helplessly on either end of the table. I made my way up the rickety ladder that led to the sleeping loft; it turned out to be just as messy as the rest of the cabin. With a good bit of house work, though, the place would be perfect. I climbed down from the loft and noticed that the sunbeams through the window now ran nearly parallel to the floor. The sun was setting rapidly, and I had to return to tell Scott the good news. I snuffed out the lantern, took one last look at our home-to-be, and bolted the door shut. Quickly, I strapped on my snowshoes, and headed for the tent. Halfway down the trail to the river, I stopped to gaze once more upon our new home. I shivered as I stood in the deep snow yet, nevertheless, I stood for a long while. It seemed as though the cabin grew directly from the earth, for it sat as naturally as any tree in the area. Its face told the tales of many changing seasons, which gave it the appearance of a great-great-grandfather with a white beard. I stood there for a long time, miles from anything, yet closer to home than I had ever felt before. In the deafening silence of the wilderness, a broad smile spanned my face. The darkening night exhaled a steady sigh, causing several puffs of snow to silently fall from the tree limbs to the forest floor. For the first time since our landing, I could honestly say, "We were home."

Quickly, I plowed through the endless ocean of snow, nearly falling with every step, for I kept looking back over my shoulder toward the cabin. Excitement made me move through the snow like a freight train and, although it was foolish, I ran nearly all the way back to our camp. I couldn't wait to reach the bivouac and break the good news to Scott. My pace gradually slowed, and for the first time, I enjoyed the untamed beauty of my surroundings. The land no longer seemed monstrous. Dangerous, yes, yet for some reason, perhaps because of the cabin, the land seemed a bit more embracing, more like home.

Soon, I saw the illuminated dome tent popping up from the frozen ground. Again the excitement overtook me, and once more I began to run through the snow. I reached the glowing tent and could smell the dinner my partner had waiting.

"Well?" Scott asked through the tent.

I was too winded to answer.

He called again, "Dave . . . you OK?" I attempted

to catch my breath in the freezing cold temperatures.

The tent door blasted open, and the only thing I could do was proudly display the thumbs-up sign, with a broad smile upon my face.

"YOU FOUND IT!"

After struggling against the elements for six days in life-threatening temperatures of 60 degrees below zero, we had finally found our home in the North . . . and that was only the beginning!

The ballad of
piggy blue Scott

'Twas sixty below 'cross the white Arctic snow,
two lads hiked forth 'neath the moon.
As they searched for their cabin those north winds were
stabbin', and O how they wished it were June.

Still they hiked through the night in the eerie moonlight,
and Cheechakos of two then were they.
And it hadn't occurred through a voice or a word,
that by God they were stuck there to stay.

So their fingers went numb and their conscience quite
dumb, and those winds O they made quite a sound.
And their stomachs did quiver as they gazed on the
river, for their cabin was nowhere around!

Well, what shall we do said the partner I knew,
it's quite clear that we cannot turn back?
And my teeth they did chatter, my mind lost its matter,
for I knew that we had to bivouac!

So we built an "A" frame ('twas more like an "A"
Shame), for its walls they allowed in the breeze.
And we froze through the night till we saw the daylight,
and we woke with a snot and a sneeze.

We were beaten and battered, our high hopes were
shattered, the only ones 'round were us two.
Then Scott stated a biggie, said "This little piggy
is frozen a frost bitty blue."

Oh great I proclaimed, this land ain't so tame,
our exhaustion had now reached its peak.
We were both scared as hell and a great silence fell,
in our shanty so scrawny and weak.

Scott left off his boot, and our voices went mute,
as we stared at the steaming gangrene.
It was gruesome and black, and it stunk up our shack.
'Twas a sight that we never had seen.

But we soon found our home, and we started to roam,
six days had now since gone past
And we thought we'd gone mad, (I believe that we
had), for something strange happened at last.

As we hiked down the path we both started to laugh,
and we saw that ol' Scott paid the cost
For somewhere on the trail (the thought turned me quite
pale) . . . Scott's big frozen piggy was lost!

Oh yes we did look and then finally shook,
at least after an hour or two.
And perhaps we would paw and find it at thaw,
but for now we gave up on Big Blue.

So when you're upset, and your maker you've met,
and your luck it has all gone to pot,
Recollect on the North, the two lads who went forth,
and the ballad of piggy blue Scott.

D. Scott

In April, during a resupply trip, Doc. examined Scott's toe and decided a skin graft was necessary. We flew out together in mid April and returned in June.

The next three months were to be the most memorable of our lives. We explored wide stretches of the Churchill River and surrounding country during days of bitter cold. We became excellent wilderness cooks, and quickly settled into the strange new rhythm that the deep and isolated wilderness had forced on our lives. We confronted long periods of tedious work, wonderful moments of great beauty, and occasional excitement with each new day. All the while, we had to contend with watching the demise of Scott's right toe as it gradually disappeared, leaving behind a rather peculiar stub.

I must give credit to Scott. After the first week of being an invalid he learned to cope with the disaster of watching his flesh rot. We soon became a two-man team once again. While daily care of the toe was part of our routine, it did not stop him from fully participating in any of the work or play. Our long treks from the cabin, which meant tent-camping at 40º below zero, continued just as we had planned. The many chores of cutting and hauling firewood; opening the ice hole and dragging buckets of water up the hill to the cabin from the river; and hunting for small game were handled by my partner and me in equal proportions.

We also came to discover the reason we had missed the cabin that first week was because we had started breaking trail from the point where the plane had dropped us off. This spot was three hundred yards from where we were supposed to have started trail blazing. In our extreme haste for great adventure this rather crucial detail had been overlooked.

Despite the traumas, neither Scott nor I would have traded the events of that first day or the days that followed for anything. In the spirit of the country, I considered that fateful first evening to be a rite of passage. We had entered the wilderness carrying backpacks full of false confidence from our safe and programmed world. We agreed that man, no matter how rich in wealth, is never the owner of all he surveys.

Scott said it best when he told me, "The Scott Power that climbed into the A-frame that night is dead! A totally different person came out the following day . . . and I think a wiser person as well."

But there was no escaping the toe. Daily care continued, and with it a certain amount of concern. We were confident the toe was not infected, but it refused to heal. We had equipped ourselves with the full medical kit Doc described in *Wilderness Medicine*, which gave us considerable depth in bandaging material. But we didn't want to run out and have to start tearing up our underwear this early in the trip.

We were both looking forward to the arrival of Doc Forgey. Without Doc's help and practical knowledge, the trip would never have gotten off the ground. He was to join us in mid-April, bringing in supplies that would last us until September, when a second visit by a larger party had been planned. A group that would include Doc, two of his friends and, hopefully, my father. Doc's mid-April visit would be our first contact with the outside since our arrival; and it would be the first that the outside would hear of us.

His visit was everything we hoped it would be. He was absolutely amazed when he heard the story of our arrival and our escapades and Doc is a person not easily impressed. We regaled Doc with the stories of our adventures, accomplishments, and screw-ups long into the night. Looking back on it, I believe Scott and I would agree the week with Doc was one of the highlights of the entire trip.

Doc waited until three days before the plane was due to pick him up to compliment Scott on the great job he had done taking care of his wound, but then informed us that we would have to return home. Scott would need a skin graft. To soften the blow, he laid out plans for a return in July to continue our adventure. This would mean extensive resupplying in Winnipeg, as we could not trust that the flour and other supplies he had brought in this trip would actually still be intact upon our return. Bears, martins, wolverines, squirrels and field mice were the potential problems, not people. We would fly in with enough supplies to last us until the September rendezvous. We would canoe out to the town of Churchill with the September party and augment what supplies we had at that time. Perhaps it would be a considerable amount more if the neighboring bears helped themselves during our absence.

Doc knew the unpredictability of the North and had planned for an emergency such as the one Scott's toe presented. He had arranged for a Beaver to pick us up, a considerably larger plane than one man would need. We climbed aboard both a plane and an emotional rollercoaster for our trip home with Doc. But July came soon enough, and the adventure continued.

"And the moose, the moose, how could I
forget, that bull with the wide-spreading
rack. He almost weighed a ton I'll bet, for he
damn near broke our backs."

D. Scott

The Hunt

The date was July 1, 1991 and once again Scott and I sat on a train rolling through the rugged Canadian wilderness. His toe had since been operated on, but neither of us were certain how it would survive the swamp crossings that would take us back to the cabin.

Fortunately, the same pilot that had flown us to the cabin in January was transporting us this time. He had heard what happened to us during our first week, and he offered to land us on the river, rather than the lake.

We informed him that no pilot in the past had dared to land even a small puddle-jumping Cessna on the river, much less an Otter.

"I'll see what I can do," he said in his heavy Canadian accent.

Two hours later, we were circling the river, and from the air I could see river stones protruding from the water. Hap, our pilot, gave us the thumbs-up sign, extended the flaps and eased back the throttle. I thought for sure we were going to die before the trip even began. Fortunately, he landed the plane safely on the river, saving us two weeks of hard work hauling gear from the swamp to the cabin, and perhaps saving Scott's toe as well.

We tethered the plane to the river bank and quickly unloaded our gear. Hap then climbed back into the cockpit and taxied the plane upstream.

The engines roared, and Scott and I held our breath as we watched the plane scream past and lift off into the sharp blue sky. He circled the plane around and did a rather dramatic fly-by, skimming directly over the tree tops and then tipping his wings as he disappeared. Scott and I stood on the bank watching as the plane faded into a tiny dot on the vast horizon. The only reminder of its presence was the water lapping on the shore in its wake. We were back.

For two days we put in long hours of hard work, cleaning the cabin, unloading gear and doing minor cabin repairs. We also pitched a tent camp a half mile downstream, which would serve as our sleeping quarters for the next two weeks. The cabin itself was far too hot and mosquito-infested to sleep in.

Three days later, while at the campsite, we were awakened by a typical northern storm. The thunder and lightning rolled up from the west, and filled the river valley with rolling echoes. A scant rain fell about the land and Scott and I spent most of the morning watching the majesty of the storm through the tent's mesh window. Soon, the cycle of the storm began to break. The thin curtain of clouds dispersed, leaving a tremendous backdrop of blue over the rugged black spruce trees.

Scott decided to spend the rest of the day swimming, reading and writing, while I decided to do some canoeing. There is much to be said about something as simple as paddling a canoe. For myself, it usually begins rather awkwardly. But once a rhythm is established, and I feel a oneness between myself, the paddle, the boat, and the water, canoeing becomes a moving meditation. The awkwardness is left in the waters behind, and what remains is nothing less than a soundless ballet across the water's surface. The mind responds to the heart, the hands respond to the mind, the paddle responds to the hands and the boat responds to the paddle. Within this cycle one is given the freedom to travel in silence over the surface of the water, and in meditation through his very soul. The late Sigurd F. Olson once said this of canoeing:

"Should you be lucky enough to be moving across a calm surface with mirrored clouds, you may have the sensation of suspension between heaven and earth, of paddling not on the water but through the skies themselves."

Slowly I paddled upstream, remembering how the cabin country had appeared when locked fast in the jaws of winter. So much had changed since then. The whispering silence of winter had turned into the joyous singing of summer. The river gurgled with life, and the warming breath of the summer wind embraced the flight of singing birds. Everywhere there was the celebration of life. In the air, in the water, and on the shore the spirit of wilderness rejoiced.

In a short time, I banked at the foot of the path that led to the cabin. I pulled the canoe to the safety of the grass and walked up the well-worn trail to the cabin's front door. Inside, the only sound was the constant drone of mosquitoes and black flies, or "bull dogs," as we preferred to call them. Unlike the changing seasons, the cabin remained the same. However, one thing did seem a bit different. The walls seemed to sag with a certain sadness. She almost seemed to be impatiently waiting for Scott and me to move back in and fill the gloomy void with laughter and the smell of coffee and wood smoke. It was almost as if our leaving had never taken place; as if going home to treat Scott's frostbite was a blurry dream.

I stood in silence, looking around the cabin that was to be our home for the next six months, for a full 180 days, and for the first time, I was homesick. I realized that the experience of returning had been as much a culture shock as exiting. Once again, we had to change our lifestyles completely. Finally, I left the cabin. I did not want to re-enter the adventure of a lifetime on a blue note. I listened attentively as the old wooden door creaked behind me, a sound that I had heard a thousand times that winter. I secured it with the rusted crowbar and returned to the canoe, looking back only once.

I decided to travel to an even more monumental spot on the map . . . the bivouac. I had not seen it in the light of the summer sun; I could only remember it drowning in a motionless wave of crystal snow. I wondered what the tiny structure would look like in the embrace of summer. To Scott and me the bivouac stood as a symbol of hard times and cold weather. Slowly, and with some difficulty, I wrestled the canoe upstream. The river's current gathered some momentum beyond the cabin, making upstream travel nothing short of hard work. I was nearing the end of the straight-away, halfway between the cabin and the bivouac, when I heard a tremendous crash in the water ahead.

Quietly I drew the boat near the shore, and edged toward the the sound. Again I heard the crash, which sounded like a huge boulder falling from the sky into the water. As I rounded the bend I saw nothing, yet the water's surface was rippled with waves. The wind was still and I was puzzled. Then, without warning, like a surfacing submarine, a bull moose rose from the water. I held my breath and grabbed my ever-present gun, for I was near enough to see the movement of his black eyes and I knew how animals behave when suddenly frightened. His antlers were in the beginning stages of growth, and his coarse black fur was slicked against his skin, defining the shape and size of his every muscle. This animal was nothing short of a giant, and I could only see half of his body; I had no idea how deep the river ran beneath his massive chest. At first, I figured he was dunking for the sake of gathering food, but seconds later he surfaced again, and I discovered the real reason for his swimming, bull dogs. They swarmed about him like a giant cloud of black velvet. I quickly discovered that my presence was not immediately threatening. In fact, he paid little attention to me. Chances are, he had never seen a human before and I'm sure he didn't care, for nothing can match the torment of bull dogs. Again he submerged and the waves from his giant body caused my canoe to rock.

The bull dogs, in a puzzled frenzy, buzzed violently, furious that they could no longer dine on the sweet nectar of moose blood. I was afraid the moose might decide to surface beneath my canoe, but he popped up some 15 yards away and ambled toward the shore, cutting through the water like an oceanliner. Those bull dogs certainly knew the value of team work. It was amazing to see them drive an animal a million times their size to the point of insanity.

The moose finally stood with his chest near the shore line, took one last look at the strange creature floating on the river then stepped upon the shore to shake himself dry. I nearly fell out of the canoe. I knew he was massive, but I would have never imagined him that huge. I guessed he weighed in excess of 1,300 pounds, and stood six-and-a-half to seven feet high at the top of his hump. His large radar-like ears twitched at the buzzing bull dogs, and his massive muscles did the same. He stared at me for awhile and then demonstrated his elusive magic. In less than ten steps, the moose melted away into the muskeg, vanishing completely. Thirteen hundred pounds of animal disappeared as though he had never been there, and he did so without a sound. I had seen deer demonstrate that trick of invisibility a thousand times back home in Indiana . . . but a moose? I was more than merely impressed, I was awestruck.

I paddled back to the campsite and told Scott what I had seen, stretching my arms skyward in demonstration of the animal's immense size. He laughed at my feeble show but enjoyed the story and shared my enthusiasm, and I was thankful I had someone to share the story with.

Many times before we left for Canada, people had asked, "Do you think you could live up there . . . alone?" and at that point, I would have said yes. But, after staying in the wilderness for an extended period, I would definitely have to say no. Yes, it would be possible, but not tolerable. One person could manage the arduous chores of daily survival on his or her own, but it would be far too difficult, Scott and I agreed, to see spectacular sights and experience unbelievable adventures without being able to share those things with someone else. I am able to share tales with other people who have been to the cabin, but they have only a slight understanding of our experience, and vice versa. There is only one person who knows how cold the first night in the bivouac was, only one person with whom I shared the joy of completing a log cabin, only one person with whom I can share the thrilling stories of the moose hunt, and only one person with whom I can talk about the many nights of Northern Lights. To this day, and perhaps for years to come, I will talk to Scott and say, "remember when" . . . and he will be the only one who will honestly be able to say, "Yeah . . . I remember." Sure, I could have lived up there alone, and so too could have Scott, yet in the end, it would have been more lonesome than adventuresome.

As we sat in the flickering firelight that evening talking about the great beast, we decided that moose meat would complement our starchy diet quite nicely. Thirteen hundred pounds of protein would easily last us the winter through. But we needed to decide wether to attempt the hunt now, in the heat of summer, or wait until old man winter began to sink his teeth into the land? After some discussion, we decided to hunt whenever the giant moose revealed himself again, which, for all we knew, might never be.

Before I continue, I would like to say this was by no means a "trophy hunt." Neither sport nor glory stood behind our reasons for pursuing this animal. We were hunting for meat, and nothing more. Doc had told us we would never get a moose for our winter meat supply, so perhaps we wished to prove him wrong. But we were not taking a life simply to prove a point. We needed meat for the winter, and fresh meat was a precious, as well as a healthy, commodity.

When I was younger, I had hunted deer quite a bit and with some degree of success. Yet this was an entirely different ball game. The land, the animals, the climate all play an essential part in the hunt and each was different than any I'd encountered before. Also, the fact that Scott and I now lived in the moose's territory would force his habits to constantly change.

For the next month, Scott and I built blinds along some of the more popular moose trails, yet the only game we brought home was a shirt of smushed mosquitoes. Unfortunately, the bugs made hunting, as well as sitting still, nearly impossible. We were soon to discover that it is neither the loneliness nor the climate, but the bugs that are the true test of man's tolerance in the North Country.

The moose hunt was looking rather hopeless until one summer night. I was sitting quietly in one of our blinds, anxiously awaiting the sound of falling hoofs. Scott was back at the cabin baking bread outside in the Dutch oven. Occasionally I could hear the faint clanking of a pot or pan, and smell the fragrance of wood smoke through the dense black spruce. The last of the day's songbirds chirped along the gnarled lips of the riverbank, and the sun was slowly ducking below the spruce-sketched horizon. I wanted to head back to the cabin for a slice of freshly baked cabin bread, yet the lack of mosquitoes and the comfort of my throne of caribou moss forced me to savor the final moments of yet another day.

At last I rose from my spot, shouldering my rifle, and headed back toward the cabin. The sky was a vibrant fiery red, and further downstream I could hear the sounds of the river gurgling over the smooth river stones, which gave me a rather peculiar idea.

When I returned to the cabin, I passed up fresh bread for a paddle, and aimed the bow of our old aluminum canoe into the setting sun. I placed Doc's Marlin .30-.30 soundlessly on the floor of the boat, and slowly pulled my way upstream. It was a gut feeling I'd had, something deep inside told me there was a moose lazily grazing around the next bend in the river . . . and sure enough, there was.

Soundlessly, I drew the boat to the bank of the river where the moose was standing. His body eclipsed the setting sun, which was now a mere sliver over the jagged tree tops. I was no more than 100 yards away, and he silently browsed, apparently unaware of, or not threatened by my presence.

I crouched as low to the ground as I possibly

could, and began my stalk, but the bugs came out again to test my patience and skill. Slowly, through the seemingly endless cloud of mosquitoes, I inched toward the moose. I wanted to be close enough for a good shot, because I questioned the knock-down power of the .30-.30.

I had closed the gap to fifty yards when the moose heaved his massive antlers up and stared directly at me. This would not have been a problem had both of my feet been planted firmly on the ground, but I was caught in mid-stride. To make matters worse, the bugs seemed to understand my predicament and launched a severe attack, going up my nose, into my eyes, and down my throat. At this point, I believe the moose realized my predicament as well, for he continued to stare, and almost seemed to laugh at my helplessness. As soon as his antlered head went back down to browse, I inhaled a tiny gnat that caused me to gag and choke. Again the moose looked up, but this time, both my feet were planted firmly on the soggy moss-covered earth.

I decided that I should get closer to the ground, so very slowly I laid on my stomach and bellied toward the moose. At thirty yards I broke a small twig beneath my knee. The moose's head quickly jerked upward and he let out a loud warning snort. I recalled the many times I'd heard deer make a similar sound, yet this snort seemed more threatening, as though the moose were saying, "Back off before I squash you like a pea!"

Slowly I stood, with the moose still staring directly at me. I eased the gun to my shoulder (simultaneously bringing back the hammer from its safety position), centered the notches on my sights between the bull's antlers, took a deep breath, and while slowly exhaling, I squeezed the trigger just like my grandfather had taught me.

The gun emitted a puff of smoke and the river valley flooded with echoes. When the smoke cleared I saw not a dead moose, but the same moose I had seen before I had pulled the trigger. He did not drop in his tracks, but stood there as if nothing had happened. He didn't even flinch, he simply stared, undaunted, and after a few seconds began to chew the grass that was left hanging over either side of his mouth. Angry that I missed, I levered, shucked the shell and aimed for a second time. Again my shot filled the valley with echoes, and this time, the moose turned and ran upstream around the riverbend. Certainly I had not missed twice, of course I was nervous, but twice? . . at thirty yards!

I waited for fifteen minutes, and then began to follow his trail, but it was too dark to see whether or not I had hit him.

My body shook with excitement. I felt certain I missed, yet what if by some miracle I had not. Unfortunately, I had no source of light with me so there was no way I could find out until the following day.

Quickly, I ran back to the canoe and paddled downstream toward the cabin. The night was beautiful, calm, still and quiet. One thousand miles away, the "real world" ran non-stop, concerning itself with the tedious details of life. Its road to success seemed narrow and over-crowded, not open and free like the winding river. Its goals seemed too animated and elusive. Too many people were selling their time for gold and giving up on their dreams.

He who dies with the most toys does not always win, he's still dead, so what difference does it make anyway? Up here, he who survives is the winner.

With so many fascinating things around me, I was constantly reminded that I wasn't missing out on all that much, and a wry smile crossed my lips when I reflected on the people who had sworn I was spending my time foolishly.

Soon, I stopped paddling and let the river carry me homeward, dipping the blade of my paddle in the water only occasionally to aim the canoe in the right direction.

I had no regrets about this adventure. I believe life is too short for regrets anyway. One of my greatest fears was passing away without ever having lived at all, without leaving something permanent of myself behind. I would not allow that to happen.

While drifting toward the cabin, I vividly recalled

one day when Scott and I were sitting near the river on a swing that we'd built. From the swing, we were fortunate enough to witness the absolute grandeur of many golden sunsets, to witness the draping curtains of green and red Northern Lights, and to be lulled by the gentle sound of the passing river. But more important than the spectacular sights from the swing were the thoughts and dreams born there. We both agreed that most of the world's problems could be solved from that very spot. Scott once told me, "We live in a vacuum . . . a place of absolute timelessness, a place of suspended animation, a place where the only moment in which to live is now." His philosophy was a good one indeed.

My thoughts drifted lazily down the river, and soon I was pulling my canoe into the safety of the stubbed willows. My heart was still racing; I thought I could see it pounding through my sweat-soaked shirt. As I hiked up the trail, I caught the faint smell of the dying embers within the fire ring. My flesh burned with the pain of a million bites from various bugs. I unloaded the .30-.30 and walked inside. The cabin was illuminated with the hissing light of our lantern, and filled with the fragrance of freshly baked bread. I sliced off a hefty hunk and stuffed it into my mouth.

Before I continue, I have to say that both Scott and I can bake delicious bread, but Scott is a master. Just like when I was little, both my mother and I could make a sandwich, yet for some reason hers always tasted better than mine, and they still do to this very day. It's all in the heart, and after tasting Scott's cabin bread, I came to the conclusion that he puts a great deal of heart into each loaf he bakes. We used the same recipes, the same ingredients, the same stove, and the same utensils, but Scott had a touch that made his bread the best.

With my mouth full, I ran up the rickety ladder and into the loft where I found Scott reading a copy of Jack London's classic *The Sea Wolf.* I nearly collapsed from suffocation, for I was out of breath, with a nose still clogged with mosquitoes and a mouth packed full with bread. At last I took a deep breath. Scott simply peered at me over the top of his book.

A rather perplexed look rested on his face and I knew, given my enthusiastic entrance, that I had some explaining to do. I told him the complete story, acting out each vital piece of information. I even displayed my stalk, hunched over in the loft of the cabin.

Scott shared the excitement, and then asked the dreaded question.

"Well . . . do you think you got him?"

I admitted because of my malfunctioning nerves, I couldn't have hit him with a Mack truck, but we still thought it best to check the area in the morning.

After my blood pressure went down, and my hands stopped shaking, I settled down with *The Silver Chair*, one in a series of seven books by C.S. Lewis (known as *The Chronicles of Narnia*), which reminds me of yet another great thing about Scott, he has a passion for good literature. I should know, I lugged seventy pounds of books over five miles of tree-choked land in frigid temperatures. However, I would drag those books to the cabin again and a million times more, for during the winter months when darkness prevailed we had little else to do other than read and write. Our library was more than impressive. With well over 165 titles, we were able to introduce each other to books and authors that in any other circumstance we most likely would never have read. Scott brought *Socrates, The Apology* and *The Notebooks of Leonardo daVinci.* He brought *Religions of the World* and *The Picture of Dorian Gray.* I brought Jack London's *The Sea Wolf,* as well as *White Fang,* both volumes containing several other short classics. I also brought *Tao Te Ching,* The *Singing Wilderness, Alive, The Prophet, Siddhartha* and *Damian.* Scott had a copy of the *Baghavad Gita* and *Echoes from a Bottomless Well.* Doc had given us several "how to" books, the best being Horace Kephart's *Camping and Woodcraft,* although Scott and I still believe that the man never skinned a moose in his life. We had lots of other books, yet my favorites to this day were *The Chronicles of Narnia.*

I climbed into my bag and continued to read *The Silver Chair.* Soon, my eyelids drooped and my chin fell upon my chest. I turned off the Coleman lantern, and watched as the color of the lantern's lingering light slowly faded from bright orange to pale blue.

Morning displayed the same colors as the fading lantern, bringing with it the singing of whiskey jacks and the chirping of our thieving neighbor, Pete the pine squirrel. Scott whipped up a batch of sourdough pancakes which we smothered in hot-buttered rum maple syrup and I brewed a pot of strong coffee. Over breakfast we discussed the moose search. I felt certain I had not killed the animal, or come even remotely close to hitting him. We decided to bring the chain saw and the axes upstream as well, to cut some firewood and make our trip worthwhile regardless.

After a thorough search, we found neither the moose, nor any blood that indicated he'd been hit. We did, however, manage to cut a great deal of firewood for the winter months that lay ahead.

August arrived with unbelievably good weather. The temperatures for nearly two weeks averaged 80 degrees. One day, the thermometer reached 100°, a 160° difference from the winter months.

We spent the days lazily, panning for gold, throwing the tomahawk, canoeing and swimming. During one week we were afraid to jump into the river because we knew a rather large and mean looking fish lurked in the depths. Scott kept catching this creature with his fishing pole, only to return it to the water for it appeared too old to eat. We figured the fish had to be upset with us and we were terrified that he might seek revenge. The old pike became known to us as "Ol' Grundy".

We also spent a great deal of time building furniture for the cabin, as well as doing minor cabin repairs and chopping more firewood.

For about one week, I felt ill. My stomach was upset, I was not hungry, and I had . . . well, I had what Scott and I came to know as the outhouse blues. I was up in the loft in my long johns, finishing off another book from *The Chronicles of Narnia*, when the door of the cabin burst open, and Scott's face appeared over my feet. "Do you feel up to skinning a moose?" he asked, with an excited gleam in his eyes.

"Hell yes!" I said as I fumbled out of the loft and into my wool pants. I ignored my sickness altogether, and quickly loaded my uncle's Marlin .308, a gun which he had graciously loaned me before my departure. I liked the old .30-.30, but I wanted the insurance that only a higher-caliber weapon could provide.

I followed Scott out the door and down to the river bank, where he pointed to the opposite shore. Sure enough, highlighted by the summer sun, the moose stood lazily browsing on supple shoots of willow. His golden robe was vibrant, and his antlers were thick with velvet. He ambled around the bend in the river, foraging until he could no longer be seen.

Quickly, I climbed into the canoe, and Scott

pushed me into the swirling amber-colored water.

Once again, as before, my heart began to race and my body began to tremble. Scott agreed to stay on the cabin side of the river, simply because it would allow him to see the moose and me at the same time. With hand signals Scott directed me to move or be still, for I could not see the moose from my position.

As quietly as possible, I banked the canoe and began walking through the soggy moss toward where the moose was last seen. My heart raced as I rounded the bend, yet much to my dismay the only thing I found was the animal's tracks. I looked at Scott who was pointing frantically up into the woods. I proceeded slowly in that direction, peering like a hungry wolf into the trees.

The water licked the bank behind my feet and the whiskey jacks and ravens filled the river valley with song, yet at that moment, the only sound seemed to be my footsteps, a sound that I did not wish to hear. Onward I pressed, staring into the thick wall of black spruce trees, intent on finding this elusive giant.

Quickly and without warning, the moose broke from his hiding place (no more than 15 feet from where I stood), and ran upstream keeping well-covered within the trees. I followed, but to no avail. Once more the moose had evaded me with very little effort, and once again he had proved me the Cheechako.

I took my time canoeing back to where Scott

stood on the shore. His eyes were wide and wild with excitement, for this was the first time he had ever seen a moose. I explained our misfortune, but Scott didn't seem to mind. Just seeing the giant animal was quite enough for him. "He'll be back," Scott assured me, "He will definitely be back."

I was equally thrilled to have seen the moose, yet I was disappointed, deprived once again of fresh meat. Something good, however, did come out of the hunt. I found a place along the river where a mudslide had exposed the bank. The ground there was nothing but smooth clay. So, for the next week I made clay pots, one of which lasted well into the winter before it exploded from the freezing temperatures.

The weather was gorgeous for the next week, and Scott and I took advantage of the sun. However, in the back of our minds we were growing concerned, anticipating the coming of winter. Because of its newness, our first winter season in Canada had been tremendous. But now we had experienced the beating heart of summer. How would we handle the transition from summer to winter? How would we handle spending 20 percent of our time outside, as opposed to the 80 percent which we were now used to.

Don't get me wrong, we both love the winter months. There is a mysterious power that hovers over the land like a huge invisible cloud. The silence, the stillness, the freshness, and the remoteness all enhance winter's charm and beauty. Woven deeply into the beauty are the bare fangs of danger, which add to the mystery and romance. Yet, to hear the joyous songs of summer and to see the cabin country bursting with life was a feeling like no other. It was a time when the days were long and the nights were cool. A time when the banks of the river were splashed with vivid colors of blooming plant life; a time when the river could be seen without ever having to open the eyes. I was afraid that when the river banks became choked with ice and her song slowly faded into winter silence, I would foolishly long for yesterday.

It was near the end of August when old mossy horns reappeared. The sun was drooping in the western horizon, and level, dust-filled beams of sunlight illuminated the cabin with a dull and fuzzy glow. From the cabin's cracked and buckled plexi-glass window I could see Scott's broken outline through the tangled trees. He stood in silent meditation, slowly reeling in his fishing line, and probably not really caring whether he caught anything or not. I knew all too well the bliss he felt, so I dared not interrupt him. I simply watched him reel in and then cast again in one fluid motion. Turning away from the window I continued my cleaning chores. The cabin door was open, and I welcomed the fresh air, drinking it in as one would drink from a pure stream.

Suddenly, Scott pounced through the open door,

and once again I could see the wild in his eyes. I had a fairly good idea of what he was going to say.

"He's back . . . He's back!" he cried, attempting to catch the breath that so quickly escaped him. "He's browsing by the feeder stream."

With the blood rushing through my veins I fumbled with the cartridges and contemplated what Scott had just told me. If indeed the moose was still near the feeder stream our chances of missing him were remote. We walked quietly along the bank of the river and peered downstream. Sure enough, the moose stood by the stream about 350 yards away. The drum of the past pounded in my heart. The absolute thrill of an honest hunt was at hand again. For generations this had been a way of life; now it was replaced with prepackaged, store-bought meat. The meaning of such a hunt had been lost, forgotten and folded away in the pages of history but now, for me, it was real. Now, I felt what men had once felt in ages past, now I felt the thrill of the hunt beating like an ancient drum deep within my very soul. Now, I felt alive!

Our plan was relatively simple and literally foolproof. Yet the wilderness had a very subtle way of turning the odds against us.

The only thing we had to do was stalk within the cover of the woods, along the river bank. The giant animal was browsing near an opening where the feeder stream met the river. From that spot, I could shoot while still under cover of the trees, and from that spot the moose would be no more than thirty feet away . . . literally foolproof.

Slowly, we made our way through the trees, moving without so much as a whisper. Again, all sights and sounds faded, leaving only Scott, myself, and the moose upon the rugged face of the earth.

Soon, we were close enough to hear him clipping the supple willow shoots between his teeth. I tried to hold my breath for fear I was making too much noise, but it was impossible. The hike to the feeder stream which normally takes a few minutes now seemed to take hours.

Scott crouched to the forest floor and pointed. Because I was behind him, I could not quite see what he was pointing at, but when I eased up next to him, I saw it was the giant beast. His ears twitched lazily, and he browsed for long periods of time without lifting his massive head to look around. He seemed completely unaware of our presence.

Scott and I moved in even closer, until finally we could see his entire body. His royal cloak shone in the sustaining red rays of falling sunlight. The fur on his belly was black as coal, while the rest of his body was a deep rich brown with traces of gray. His palm-like antlers stretched first outward, and then skyward as if holding up the very sun itself. They had grown tremendously since our last encounter. His nostrils dilated with every breath, and occasionally, but not in a threatened manner, he would inhale deeply with his head high to test the wind, only to exhale air that proved no trespassers were in the area. Fortunately for us, the wind was blowing from north to south, and we stood south of the moose, rendering him oblivious to our presence.

He continued to browse on the age-twisted face of land until he stood at last on the very edge of the feeder stream. He was 30 feet away, facing Scott and me, with his head down. I brought the gun slowly to my shoulder. The weapon's weight seemed to multiply while poised in its shooting position and my knees felt as though they would give out at any moment. Holding my breath, I peered through the scope, and for a moment I thought perhaps the scope was covered with dirt, for I could not see through its window. I quickly realized that it wasn't dirty at all, but completely filled by the moose's giant flaring nostrils.

I could already smell fresh moose steaks cooking over an open fire. I could visualize them sprinkled with a delicate layer of seasonings and being graciously licked by an open flame. My mouth watered, and my stomach growled, and I slowly inched the gun upward. Soon, both of the moose's eyes rested on either edge of the scope's horizontal cross-hairs. When the cross-hairs were steady and centered upon his forehead, I took a deep breath, slowly exhaled, and squeezed the trigger.

I'm sure the echoes traveled for miles, yet I don't even recall the ring of the initial shot. In fact, I can hardly recall the entire incident, with the exception of one chain of events. The moose made a loud snorting noise, heaved himself backwards, and then trotted to the treeline some 20 feet away from where he originally stood.

Quite frankly, I consider myself to be rather accurate with a weapon. Yet, one minute after the shot, the moose still stood. Either we were staring at a ghost, or I missed the shot . . . again.

Missed the shot? No way, that was impossible! His forehead had filled my entire scope, I was thirty feet away, and I knew from shooting two days prior that my sights were dead on . . . literally. But there he stood breathing heavily, alive and well.

Quickly, and in a rather angered fashion, I raised the gun once more to my shoulder, took a deep breath, slowly exhaled, and squeezed the trigger.

"CLICK." That was the report of the gun . . . click! My uncle's .308 is a high-powered semi-automatic rifle. It will hold five rounds in the clip, and one in the chamber. The gun should have ejected the spent cartridge and filled the chamber on its own, but it hadn't. For the first time the gun had jammed. I know what you're thinking, "Oh great, another story of the one that got away." But it's true. No sooner had I finally landed a shell in the chamber did the moose melt soundlessly into the dense cover of the trees. By now the sun had fallen, and my awareness of the sights and sounds around us became more acute.

"I don't believe it!" Scott cried, not angered by my inaccuracy but truly amazed that I missed. He really didn't believe it . . . nor did I.

We allowed the moose twenty minutes (well, maybe five, but it seemed like twenty), and then I had Scott walk up the feeder stream approximately thirty yards and cut into the woods. I was hoping that he might flush the moose out into the open of the river bank, but it never happened. While Scott was in the woods, I thought of the foolish situation into which I had thrown him. It was dark, he had no gun, he was pursuing the largest wild animal in North America, and that animal was most likely wounded. I'd had some pretty stupid ideas before, but this one took the cake.

I began walking quietly into the tangled forest, when suddenly I heard the moose breathing in a very abnormal fashion. He sounded much like Darth Vader from the Star Wars movies. I met Scott; he also heard the strange breathing, almost as if the moose was wheezing. We began to follow the noise, being careful not to create any noise ourselves. The closer we got, the louder the noise became, and the louder the noise became, the more frightened we got. I had the gun poised and off safety, ready for anything out of the ordinary. I don't recall how full the moon was, but I do remember that it was present that night, for in my mind's eye I can see that grayish-blue forest painted with long black shadows.

Finally I stopped. The noise was very near. As the moose inhaled and exhaled, the hair on the back of my neck rose and fell, like waves on an empty shoreline. He had to be visible; it almost seemed as though we could feel the heat from his very breath. The noise seemed to fill the black woods with haunting sounds that were growing louder. Scott and I stood for a long time, attempting to visually pierce the darkness, yet we saw nothing.

I decided to step forward, and upon doing so, the moose revealed himself. He was no further than fifteen feet away, and perhaps I could have shot him. Instead, I simply stood and watched him as he vanished in the gnarled, shaggy spruce trees. I was too awestruck to breathe, let alone aim a gun with accuracy. When I snapped out of my trance, I asked Scott to help me feel the ground. Because it was fairly cold that night, I figured the ground where the moose had rested would still be warm, and sure enough it was. He had lain there for several minutes, and at least thirty minutes had passed since I had fired the initial shot. We wanted to see if we could find any traces of blood. But because of the darkness, we couldn't tell a drop of blood from a shadow. Scott ran back to the cabin to get the other gun, a lantern, and some blaze orange trail-marking tape, while I sat near the spot where the moose had been. Soon, the sound of Scott's footsteps were swallowed by the swamp and I was alone. Once again, the sound of the moose's labored breathing shattered the silence of the night, and I can honestly say that it was quite scary. I sat with my back against a large spruce tree and clutched my gun with my finger on the trigger. I began to dwell on the events of the past hour. There was no way I had missed that moose; he should be dead by now . . . but he wasn't. I was disappointed in myself, and I knew right then and there that my grandfather would never let me live this one down. Again I heard the moose inhale and exhale deeply and slowly, in the same manner as before. And then, a dreadful thought entered my mind. Was he suffering? When hunting, the kill must be as quick and as clean as possible. I could only hope that he wasn't.

When Scott returned, I fired up the lantern and inspected the ground where the moose had been laying. There was not a speck of blood anywhere to be seen. The only thing to do was go back to the cabin and wait until first light to continue the search. We did not want to pursue him now, and risk pushing him deeper into the swamp.

Scott and I back-tracked to the feeder stream, marking the trail with orange tape every twenty feet.

Back at the cabin, we relived the thrilling episode over and over, re-enacting several of the highlights. Our excitement filled the cabin, yet it was tempered by our belief that the moose we so respected and revered was now in the swamp dying a slow and painful death. Our bearded faces masked the concern with excitement, yet we felt remorse at the thought.

"By the way," Scott said. "As I was hiking up that feeder stream, I got a funny feeling. I mean, there I was in the forest, with only a Swiss Army knife for protection, pursuing the largest wild game animal in North America, and for all I knew, he was wounded, or at least really pissed off." He ended with a smile.

"Well," I said in jest, "look at it this way, had we both been armed, what do you suppose would have happened if we startled each other out there in the black woods. We would have blown each other's brains out!" I laughed. "All in the name of fresh meat!" Scott added. Although the joke was rather demented, it seemed to break the tension, and calm the excitement. Scott worked with the fire, and I decided to go to the river for another bucket of water. I pulled on my old smoke-scented sweater, and crawled through the tiny door that led to the outside world.

Quietly, I closed the door behind me, tiptoed over to the wood pile, and peered into the open sky. Silence. The sky, the land, the cabin, even the river which usually sang so boldly seemed to whisper away into the night. The entire country appeared to be meditating. I wondered, "what was it thinking?"

I ambled down the path that led to the river bank.
Because the bend in the river near the cabin was so
broad, the water flowed very slowly. On some nights
the river looked like a glass-topped lake. Upon its
mirrored surface, I could see deep into space without
ever looking up. In the distance, I heard the whistle of
wings and suddenly two loons bolted past like two jet
fighters flying in formation. The river captured their
reflection only to quickly let it go. I couldn't cast the
bucket into the river as I had always done in the past,
but rather dipped it in slowly. The ripples disturbed the
heavens, but only for a moment, then all was still once
more. Smiling, I turned and hiked up the trail toward
the cabin, allowing the water from the over-filled bucket
to splash on my legs. I could see the smoke from our
silhouetted stove-pipe, puffing into the pale sky. In the
window, I could see the light of our lantern, and beyond
that I saw Scott walking back and forth from the stove to
the supply shelves, preparing something to eat. It was a
beautiful sight, a dark sky, a dark cabin, and a single light
streaming from a single window onto the forest floor. A
single light coming from a little cabin miles from
anywhere. It was a warming sight that made me feel at
home, that made me feel secure even while nestled
within the gaping jaws of the unknown. My arm was
growing tired from the weight of the water bucket, and
after listening once more to the overwhelming silence, I
returned to the cabin.

Waiting for the mechanics to heat the plane's engine, the pilot would not fly until it "warmed up" to 40º below.

When the bush plane disappeared over the horizon, we heard for the first time, the great silent voice of the North.

Waving goodbye to the pilot.

Standing in front of the bivouac where we spent our first and coldest night (60º below). This picture was taken three months after that evening.

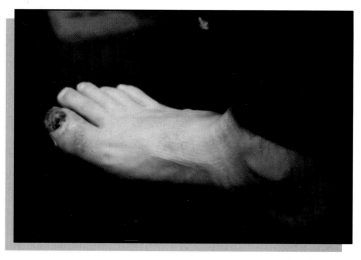

Scott's frostbitten toe, the result of our first night.

Heading back down the Little Beaver
after an unsuccessful search for the cabin.

This is how the cabin looked when I first saw it.
I stopped to take this picture just before heading
back to tell Scott the good news.

The entrance to Dr. Forgey's cabin. A true home away from home.

The outhouse. Everything you set out to do in the North requires great courage and determination.

The pantry I made for the inside of Doc's cabin. Some of my mother's recipes are tacked to the inside of the door.

A swim in Paradise Creek is an indescribable experience. Chances are Scott and I were the first people to swim in this stream. Seeing it for the first time Doc Forgey said: "Kid, this is paradise." From then on it was Paradise Creek.

The first logs for our new cabin are ready to be pulled ashore.
They were cut one half mile up stream.

Scott carrying supplies from
the canoe to the cabin.

Scott struggling to get another log up the hill.

Chopping another notch in preparation
for the third course of logs.

Adding moss between one of
the notches to help make the
cabin air tight.

We set the floor at a diagonal for
no reason other than to give our
cabin a touch of class.

Taking time out to complete a journal entry.

Fitting the west-facing window.

Using Doc's chainsaw to ready the
logs for a window.

84

We camped near the cabin while its construction took place.
Each night we would look out of the tent in admiration of
our accomplishments.

The only time we canoed to Churchill was to retrieve nails,
hinges and plexi-glass for our cabin project.

Our cabin at Paradise Creek. Neither of us had ever worked so hard
on anything. Never had anything given us such great satisfaction.

This picture was taken two days before we moved in. The
cabin took 19 days to complete, and by this time excitement
and exhaustion filled the air.

Two photos of the Little Beaver taken from roughly the same spot in front of our cabin. The top photo was taken in October and the bottom in August. The spot where Paradise Creek empties into the Little Beaver can be seen in foreground of the lower picture.

A moment of song on a swing
we built in front of Doc's cabin.

Scott and I spent many hours
panning for gold. The sum of
our findings could be used as a
filling for a small tooth. Despite
our "bad luck" we were rich.

Since we lived so near
the river, fish became
an important part of
our diet.

A typical dinner consisting of bread, pasta, tea and, if we were lucky, chocolate.

Pikes cooking Cree style over a small fire.

Scott mixing up another batch of his famous sourdough cabin bread.

My heart was pounding as I approached this giant creature. I felt neither joy nor guilt, but rather more a part of my surroundings.

Putting the last pieces of meat into our refrigerator. This box, dug deep into the permafrost, held 500 pounds of meat, enough for the winter months ahead.

Skinning, quartering, moving and butchering the moose took three days.

To insure that nothing was wasted, we smoked the smaller
remaining pieces.

To show our respect for this noble animal, we built a tripod
and suspended a willow hoop over the spot where his remains
are buried . . . it still stands today.

One week after Scott and I shot the moose, my father came
in with Dr. Forgey on a re-supply trip. This was, without
question, one of the great highlights of the trip.

After several restless hours tossing, turning, Scott and I managed to get some sleep. Yet, even while resting, the questions continued to lurk. Did I hit the moose? Was he wounded and suffering? Was he dead? If indeed he was dead, how many bears were tearing at his flesh while I lay in bed worrying? Sleep was not an easy task that night, but as I said before, it did eventually get the best of both of us.

I was awakened by the sound of Scott's laughter. Slowly my eyes opened, and I asked him what was so funny. He explained, attempting not to laugh.

"It was the scratching on the floor boards that awakened me this morning. When my eyes opened, I found myself staring directly into the eyes of our neighbor Pete. He sat near the corner of the loft, munching away on a hunk of bread twice his size. I blinked in the sunlight that came through the loft window and when I did, the squirrel dropped his bread and dove for the nearest escape hole. I watched the hole, knowing that a squirrel like Pete would never leave behind a hunk of bread that size. Soon, his nose poked through the escape hole, he grabbed the piece of bread, threw his gears into reverse, and scrambled backwards towards the hole. But the bread was far too large for the rather small escape route, and it nearly pulled Pete's teeth clean out of his mouth when it got caught in the hole's frame. He gave up for a second, but came back a little later for his loot.

"I know they say that animals can't reason, but after observing him, I think differently. He stared at the bread for some time, and then rotated it in his paws until it would fit through the small opening. Sorry my laughing woke you up, but it was pretty funny."

Before breakfast, I grabbed the water bucket and headed down to the river. I could see, through a transparent curtain of trees, long fingers of mist gently stroking the water's placid surface. Ever so subtly, the sun lifted the mist from the autumn-colored banks of the river. To this day, I can't begin to count the times I'd stood somewhere along that shore and held my breath.

Again, instead of casting the empty bucket into the water, I slowly dipped it, attempting to disturb as little as possible. Any loud noise at that moment would have been a sacrilege.

My eyes followed the course of the winding river until they fell upon the feeder stream. "Somewhere," I thought, "somewhere within that forest lurks the answer to last night's mystery. Somewhere within that darkened wood is the moose." With a full bucket that shifted my weight heavily to one side of the trail, I walked toward the cabin.

Over a breakfast of freeze-dried eggs and coffee, Scott and I discussed the events of the previous night and how we would handle the hours ahead. Even though we were anxious to begin the search, we talked for more than an hour, finishing our conversation with a final slug of coffee and a one-ounce chunk of chocolate.

Grabbing the necessary provisions, we headed for the old Grumman canoe and aimed its bow toward the bubbling feeder stream. The mist had since been stolen by the sun and the golden water rippled and sang happily with the lick of each paddle stroke. Here and there the subtle signs of autumn were becoming more distinct. The invisible hand of nature was gently painting the land with a few select colors. A solitary touch of gold highlighted the entire shoreline, and above geese could be heard heading south to evade the bitter winter months. Fall was not completely upon us yet, but its signature sights, smells and sounds made us realize it was not far away.

The keel of our aluminum canoe made a grinding noise as its bow slid into the sandbar, and Scott jumped out to pull the bow further onto the beach. From where we stood, I could see the pieces of orange trailing tape hanging loosely from shaggy limbs, leading into the thick wall of trees. Like hounds, we began tracking the moose. We first studied the area in which he had stood when I had initially fired. There was an explosion in the soft mud, where the moose quickly spun and ran up the hill, yet no blood was visible. Slowly, we followed his tracks deeper and deeper into the woods, until we arrived at the spot where the last piece of tape hung. Again, we found no blood. We traveled deeper into the woods. Suddenly, I thought I heard the strange wheezing sound of the moose breathing as he had the previous night. Cautiously, I continued deeper into the brush toward the sound. I knew that while on a game trail, a hunter's mind can play tricks, making him believe in something that isn't even there.

This, however, was no trick. Our next step brought the perfectly camouflaged moose to his feet no more than 10 yards from us. He wasted no time in retreating deeper into the forest, and then all was silent.

Either of us could have easily shot him at that point, yet we simply stood and watched him dissolve into the lush woods, too dumfounded to move. After several minutes, Scott and I continued our search. We decided to split up. I traveled up the feeder stream toward Landing Lake, and Scott traveled the shoreline of the river.

One hour led to two, two hours led to four, and four hours led to five. I had walked nearly six miles into the bush in search of the prehistoric-looking monster, to no avail. Even if we did find him and kill him, we would never be able to pack all that meat back to the cabin in one night. Thirteen hundred pounds meant at least 12 trips, and 12 trips at this distance meant at least 7 or 8 days. So at night, one person would have to guard the meat from hungry bears. Quite frankly, I didn't believe any meal was worth that much toil in the heart of the swamp, so upon reaching Landing Lake, I turned and headed back toward the cabin.

Along the way, I shot a plump young spruce grouse. Although I was thankful for the bird, I was hoping for something more along the lines of a three-pound moose steak. Also on the trail, I found the components of a weather balloon, as well as part of the balloon itself. In a rather peculiar way, the instrument reminded me that there was indeed such a thing as "civilization" outside of our vacuum.

"I heard a shot, did you get him?" Scott asked with excitement.

I held up the spruce grouse and smiled weakly.

"We've got as great a chance of hitting that moose as we do finding a weather balloon in the swamp!" I replied, holding up the tangled nest of strings, wires, and rubber.

Scott laughed, and together we walked to the cabin. He had "patrolled" up and down the banks of the river in search of the ghost animal . . . again to no avail. We were both exhausted, and we were both depressed, but at least we would have grouse for dinner.

Back at the cabin, I began cleaning the bird. The sun slowly eased down behind the tree tops, and the beating heart of the north country seemed to slow its pace. Within the thick carpet of moss on the forest floor, I could see scattered tinges of orange, red, and gold, accented by the level rays of sunlight. The wilderness exhaled a lonely sigh and its breath felt cold, like a splash of water upon my face. Before entering the cabin,

I scanned the now-dark woods. Somewhere . . . somewhere out there was the giant moose. Once more he had evaded our attack. After today, I believed that we would never see him again. Of course, I was wrong.

September 4, 1991. The day was windy, yet fairly warm. I decided, because of the wind, to build a sail for the canoe. This was something I'd read about, but never tried. I fashioned a rectangular frame for the sail from four freshly cut saplings, to which I attached a canvas fly from an old tent of ours. The sail would lie flat on the top of the canoe, and then, when the sailor was ready, it could be hoisted by pulling on cords that were attached to the top of the frame. I wasn't sure how the contraption would work, but it was worth a try.

I pushed the canoe into the open water, and paddled toward the middle of the river. The bottom of the sail's frame was wedged tightly outside the gunwales of the boat, so its fit was snug and secure. Once in the middle of the river, I pulled on the sail strings, and instantly it filled with the billowing wind. The canoe danced across the surface of the water. Under the arm of my free hand, I held a canoe paddle like a rudder to steer the boat. For the first time I was traveling upstream with no effort, moving faster than a man could run. I was ecstatic. The bow of the boat slapped the rippling water as its speed increased, and every now and then a splash of cold water would jump up and lick my face.

I was turning around for another run downstream when I saw him. The sound of my descending sail hitting the canoe had scared the moose from his hiding place. He was on the opposite shore, and it was obvious that we had never hit him by the way he ran.

Quickly, I sailed the canoe into the bank on our side of the river and ran, full steam, to the cabin's front door. The battle cry that was growing more and more popular rang out again within the tiny room. "He's back . . . he's back!" For a brief instant, the cabin exploded with life. The guns quickly came from the gun rack, and more ammunition ended up on the cabin's floor than in the guns themselves. Knives were sheathed and harnessed, and mukluks were laced tightly. We arrived at the bank of the river just in time to see the moose vanish around a bend on the opposite shore. As we shoved off, I heard Scott whisper, "That's him all right, he's back!"

By this time Scott and I could power a boat as one man; we were completely synchronized (and we didn't even have to sing a voyageur song to do so). We paddled the canoe silently to the opposite shore.

After we landed, Scott and I crouched low and stalked around the bend where we last saw the magnificent beast . . . but he was gone. I asked Scott to walk downstream 100 yards, and then to cut into the woods and walk upstream, making plenty of noise in the process. I would wait upstream in hopes that Scott would scare the moose my way. Our chances of flushing the moose were slim, but we had no choice.

One minute faded to three minutes, then three to six, then six to ten; my hopes sank into the mud beneath my feet. Once again, we would be deprived of fresh meat.

Then, ever so faintly, I could hear something coming through the brush. I figured it was Scott, but soon the sound was roaring like a jet engine, and in the woods before me appeared the moose. The sound of his thunderous hooves dopplered like a passing freight train, and after pausing for a moment, I charged into the woods and followed the towering animal. I could no longer see him, but I could hear his massive body crashing through the tangled brush. And then, suddenly, the noise stopped. I continued walking softly through the woods, until I came to where the trees met the shoreline. The moose was (diagonally) one hundred and fifty yards away on the opposite side of the river shaking droplets of water from his thick coat. In less than a minute he swam from one bank to the other.

Once again, the gun became heavy in my hands. I did not wish to simply hit the animal. I did not wish to see such a magnificent creature run deep into the swamp and suffer. What I wanted was a kill, one shot, quick and clean, plain and simple.

Experience told me not to attempt a shot at such a distance. Although it was probably only a few seconds, it seemed as though the moose and I stared at each other forever on that vacant shoreline, just the two of us, man and beast. And then . . . and then the butt of the gun rested upon my shoulder, and my right eye was peering at the moose through the circular window of the scope.

I do recall telling myself that I was not going to take the shot; I do not recall saying to myself, "You can do it . . . take aim and shoot!"

But there I was, poised and inhaling deeply, prepared to terminate this animal's breathing for eternity. I slowly released my breath while squeezing the trigger. But I did not squeeze the trigger as I had been religiously taught by my grandfather, rather, I pulled it, causing the barrel of the gun to jerk downward and to the right. Luckily, I paid greater attention to one of his other lessons in the shooting of a firearm, for in my haste, I had forgotten to take the gun off safety.

Quickly, the gun was readied, and for a second time, I raised it to its proper firing position. Like a leaf releasing melting snow from its back, I fired my best shot. Although it may sound strange, the shot seemed to fire itself. I knew before I could even see over the end of the gun barrel; I knew the moose was dead!

I do not recall the sound of the river, nor do I recall the echo of the report booming through the valley. I do not recall the ever-present sound of singing birds, nor do I recall the whispers composed by autumn's breezes. In that brief moment of sheer adrenaline intensity, the only thing I heard, and felt, was thirteen hundred pounds of solid animal slamming down on the shoreline, and then all was silent. When the smoke cleared and my senses returned, I could see the moose across the golden swirling water. He did not kick, he did not twitch. I had dropped him where he stood, a one shot kill, quick and clean, plain and simple. My grandfather would have been proud!

Soon, other sights and sounds began to return to my numbed senses and I could hear Scott coming up the river bank. "Did ya get him ? . . Did ya get him?" he called.

I stood with a smile painted upon my face, and an outstretched finger pointing toward the opposite bank of the river.

We spent the next five minutes back-slapping, high-fiving, hee-hawing, and bear-hugging. After several months of hunting the elusive prey, our patience and persistence had finally paid off. To Scott and me that day was Thanksgiving. We now had our winter's supply of meat.

We climbed into the canoe and headed back to the cabin for knives, towels, a small hatchet, and a camera.

When all the gear was loaded in the canoe, we slowly paddled upstream. We approached the silent animal much like one would approach a 1,300 pound firecracker that hadn't blown. Never had I seen such a magnificent creature. The moose lay completely still on a bed of tall grass. For the first time in all my years of hunting I felt no remorse, no sense of guilt. What I had done here was expected in the eyes of wilderness. What I had done was natural in the perpetual cycle of life and death.

Cautiously, I stepped toward the giant bull with my finger over the trigger of my uncle's gun. The moose seemed dead, but because of his immense size, I was not going to gamble. I was no more than two paces away when the great animal sat up with his forelegs outstretched before him. I staggered backwards, and nearly dropped the rifle on my foot. Without delay, I raised the gun to my shoulder and shot the moose directly behind the ear.

The giant animal kicked wildly, and I fired again for fear that he would kick his way into the river. After that, all was silent. I walked toward the moose and nudged him with the barrel of my gun. At last, he was truly dead.

Skinning, cleaning and butchering the animal was a major task. The first thing we had to do was roll him onto his back. Both Scott and I conjured all of our strength and heave-hoed until I thought all of the veins in my neck and head would explode. Because his back was so angular, we had to prop him up with logs to prevent his rolling over.

I drew my knife and paced from one end of the moose to the other as if I didn't know where to begin. I'd done this before but never had I skinned an animal so large. After the initial incision however, I remembered everything.

Once his chest and stomach cavity were cleaned, we had to "quarter" him. The job was not an easy one, nor a clean one for that matter. By the time it was completed Scott and I were exhausted and covered with blood.

Next, we had to transport the meat to the cabin. It took both Scott and me to carry a single hind quarter. We nearly sank the canoe when we overloaded it with meat, and although we didn't sink the boat, we did manage to blow out one of the thwarts because of the tremendous pressure placed on the gunwales.

Several strenuous hours later all of the meat, as well as the hide, was at the cabin. We were both exhausted, and thinking of going to bed, yet one major task remained. Scott drew his knife and custom-carved a steak to fit our largest pan. I removed the animal's tongue, for to the Native Americans, this was the finest cut of meat on any large animal.

Our Thanksgiving steak was outstanding, and Scott and I ate it as a wolf would eat a fresh kill. I don't believe the steak could have been categorized as having been cooked to the stage of rareness. Our faces were ringed with blood when we were done.

As for the tongue . . . well, I mean no disrespect to the Native Americans, and I certainly mean no disrespect to the moose, but I ended up feeding that piece of tradition to the martins, due to my lack of knowledge on how to prepare such a delicacy.

After dinner, we opened a bottle of our finest Scotch and raised our our tin cups in honor of the moose. From that day forth he has been spoken of with as much respect and reverence as the bivouac. And if you ever get a chance to visit Doc's cabin yourself, you will find a willow hoop suspended from a tripod and placed above the grave where his bones lie.

The Cabin

"I'll only be gone a week or so," I told Scott as I loaded up the canoe on that hot day of August 19, 1991.

During our ten-month stay in the wilderness, Scott and I frequently went on solo trips away from the cabin. These trips would last anywhere from two to ten days, regardless the season. Our mode of transportation was either foot, snowshoe, ski, or canoe. We would travel one to ten miles away from the cabin, and although there was no specific reason for leaving, each of us hoped to discover some magical place never before seen. Our attempts never once failed.

It was important for us to venture away from the confines of the cabin, and from each other. In a way, camping out helped to re-energize our minds. These camping excursions never meant we were upset with each other; they were simply a way of cleansing the mind, and of getting away. Plus, there was no greater joy, no greater sense of belonging, than upon returning "home," propping your feet up by the stove with a cup of coffee, and re-living your great adventure with your partner.

So there I was, on the threshold of a major campout preparing to . . . well, preparing to go camping. My Duluths were packed, my canoe (as well as my gun) was loaded, and my map was unevenly folded and stuffed into my pocket. I had planned originally to stay away for at least two weeks, and to travel as far upstream as I possibly could. However, I quickly became side-tracked by a project that for Scott and me eventually turned into an accomplishment that could be likened to walking on the moon.

Scott pushed the stern of our trusty canoe into the swirling water, said good-bye, and, as we both had always done when the other would leave, told me to watch my step. I told him to do likewise.

The journey began as all upstream travel begins slowly, painfully, and psychologically taxing. To begin with, there was a fairly strong head wind. Scott and I had a running joke about the wind at the cabin. It would be calm while we were on land, but once the bow of the canoe hit the water, its direction would change, and its velocity increase. It never failed, and this day was no exception.

I was in the stern of the boat and my gear was stowed in the bow. Even though I had the canoe balanced to some extent, the wind blew the bow of the boat 180° across the water. Finally, I climbed between the thwarts, which I've always hated to do, and kneeled in the middle of the boat. In spite of the difficulties, I enjoyed every second of hard work.

Soon, I was beyond the site where Doc had cut the logs for his cabin, and around the following bend, I could see the eerie outline of the bivouac. This particular bend in the river, to Scott and me, had become sacred. It seemed as though a mysterious force surrounded the entire area, for each time we canoed past, we fell into silence. We could be talking and laughing, but when we drifted beyond a certain point, our laughter melted away into the black woods, and our breaths were held. That particular night of January 29, 1991, could have gone either way, and Scott and I were reminded of that each time we canoed past.

The river beyond the bivouac gathers a great deal of speed. It is quite possible for one man to canoe up that stretch, but it is also rather tricky. As any canoeist knows, one should normally stay along the shore when paddling upstream. In this stretch of water, a large rock protrudes from the shoreline three feet into the waterway. To pass the rock, I had to first angle the bow of the canoe toward the middle of the river. This maneuver, due to the fact that the river ran rapidly around the rock, had to be made quickly and accurately, or else the boat would end up speeding down the emerald rapids, perpendicular to the river's banks.

Rather than wrestle with the river, I decided to "track" the canoe upstream. I attached two lengths of rope to the canoe, one to the bow and one to the stern, and used lines to walk, or "track," the canoe upstream. To pass shoreline obstacles, I pulled the stern in closer to shore and allowed the bow to drift, angling out into the river. The canoe then tracked upstream, with the side-wash ferrying it around any obstacles on or near the shoreline. I had to take precautions however, for tracking is not as simple as it sounds. Slipping on a rock, capsizing the canoe, or losing control of the boat are the end results of poor technique or bad luck. It is a maneuver recommended for two people as opposed to one, yet one can manage.

Soon, I was around the rock and back in the boat, paddling with no particular destination in mind. The wind persisted in its attempts to force me downstream, and the bugs siphoned blood from any square inch of exposed flesh they could find. Nonetheless, I continued my journey. The river slowed a bit along the shore, and far to the northwest I could see an approaching storm. Also to the west, directly in front of me, was a single tree that stood high above the rest of the forest. Following its trunk to the ground I saw what appeared to be a feeder stream, and then I remembered back to February 2, 1991. This was the very feeder stream that showed us the way to the cabin, and that was the tree I had climbed and spotted the tiny lake. As I approached, I could see the feeder stream more clearly, and on the corner where it met the river, the bank rose fifteen feet, leveling off for a perfect camping site. I banked the canoe and began to explore the area. The giant tree was on the opposite side of the feeder stream, and after crossing the water I walked up to the tree's massive trunk. I could see, looking up, the trail I had made through the twisted limbs toward the top. Bark was peeled away, limbs were snapped, and surprisingly, I even found the handkerchief that I had lost at the base of the tree that winter.

After making several passes around the massive trunk, I wove up the feeder stream. The place seemed to have emerged from the pages of a fairy tale. Without a doubt, it was the most beautiful place I had ever seen. The feeder stream averaged five feet across, and its deep waters ran fast, cold and clear. The trees along its shore were massive in comparison to the rest of the trees in the area, and they grew fairly far apart, allowing me to see much further than normally possible. Here and there the stream's banks widened to form swirling pools ten to twelve feet across. Sometimes these pools had tiny islands within them on which a tree or two would grow, but more often than not they were clear.

I could no longer stare at the beautiful golden stream; I had to immerse myself in its waters. I stripped off my sweaty clothes and plunged into one of the icy pools of water. For a moment I lost my breath, but soon my body became acclimated to the water and I swam for a long time, knowing that I was quite possibly the first person to ever swim in this stream. In some parts of the pool the water was over my head, but for the most part, it was no more than five feet deep. I spent the better part of an hour swimming to the pool's floor and surfacing with handfuls of rocks and sand, looking for any flakes of gold.

Finally, I climbed out of the pool and stood on the shore drip-drying, while the bugs buzzed around me in search of the perfect artery. Once dressed, I returned to where my canoe was beached, grabbed my Duluths, and headed up the hill to set up camp. To the west, I could see the storm rolling down the river. It appeared it would not blow over my camp, for it was heading in a more southerly direction. Behind the storm, I could see the sun falling into the horizon, its golden rays vainly attempting to pierce the falling curtain of rain. The view from the hilltop was more than spectacular, it was awesome. Although the hill wasn't very tall, I could see the entire valley below. The river came in from the west, and went out to the east, moving like a giant lazy python, giving life to everything upon its shores.

I turned to my gear and began preparing my camp. Scott and I continued to use the same tent we had used our first cold week in the North, even though it did not have any shock chords. It looked like it had been through a battle, and I suppose it had, but it continued to fight the elements like a champ.

After struggling with both the tent and the bugs, I soon had shelter and the food was steaming over an open fire. I could hear the storm, which seemed to be following the path of the river, and I realized that it was not going to evade me. I wolfed down the final scraps of my meal and secured the tent. I could tell from its sound that this storm meant business.

Its voice grew louder, and its winds became more overwhelming. The tent walls began to billow, forcing me to sit in the center with my feet anchoring the corners of the floor, and my hands pushing up on the ceiling. I thought for sure my tent would end up being blown through the woods. Yet my tent and I continued to hang on, fighting for life.

The sound of the storm was now deafening. I kept my fists propped into the ceiling as I waited for the tent walls to give up the battle and collapse. Suddenly something crashed into the knuckles of my right hand. The intense pain made me pull my hand back quickly, causing the tent wall to droop under the tremendous pressure of the winds. Before I could figure out what hit me, something smashed into the knuckles of my left hand. For a moment, I thought the wind was blowing dead tree limbs down upon my tent. Then, with a loud "clank," I heard one of the mystery objects hit my canoe. Hail! Not small hail stones, however, these were huge. I grabbed my boots, slipped them over my hands for protection, and continued to hold the tent together. I thought for sure the tent would be torn to shreds, but it continued to "serve and protect" as it had so faithfully in the past. One of the tent windows was partially open, and through its mesh screen I witnessed the absolute power of raw nature. The scene was spectacular, but because my hands were occupied, I could not close the window to keep out the rain. The rain and hail smashing into the aluminum canoe sounded like machine-gun fire, and I wondered if my boat would be blown into the water and carried downstream, for I did not have it secured in any way to the bank.

The storm slowly drifted downstream, and silence once again gripped the land. I removed my boot mittens and poured some iced tea from one of my water bottles into a large tin Sierra cup. Thanks to the storm, I had the distinct pleasure of having tea "on the rocks," with ice cubes ranging in size from that of a marble to that of a golf ball. Outside, trees were uprooted, limbs were scattered, the bottom of my canoe was covered with dents, and my tent seemed to sag as if praying for mercy.

I strolled around the river bank and surveyed the damage. Never before had I witnessed a storm strike with such power and vengeance, and I have seen a few good ones. The great thing about this storm was that I had experienced it from inside a tent. Had I nothing over my head, I would have been sprawled out on the forest floor with massive head traumas. Lazily, I walked to the mouth of the feeder stream, savoring the aromas brought about by the storm. Everything smelled so fresh; everything looked so clean and new. I returned to my tent, which seemed to beg for an early retirement, and burrowed into my damp sleeping bag. The level of excitement that boiled in my veins temporarily prevented sleep, but soon my heartbeat slowed to match the tempo of the wilderness and my eyelids became heavy with sleep.

I arose early the following morning, and tunneled outside through the tent's door. The scene was again spectacular, this time complete with two Canada geese swimming in the river. For a long while, I stood in silence atop the small knoll and gazed into the river valley at my feet. In the east the sun was climbing over the tangled mass of limbs that guarded the level horizon, creating long westward shadows that silently ran away into the forest. The river, in no particular hurry, rolled along on its journey to the ocean, and the song birds sang praise to the breaking of a new day. Never before had I seen the wilderness in such a pristine state. I realized that all places wild are, in their own way, pristine, yet for some reason, perhaps because of its remoteness, this place was different. This land upon which I stood was much more than another mark on the map. This place was powerful, and to Scott and myself, it became truly sacred ground.

As I walked the perimeter of my camp site an idea suddenly came to mind. I climbed into the canoe and headed toward the cabin to retrieve some tools.

My original intention was to build a sauna on the bank of the river where my camp was. However, the idea grew into something much larger.

Many Native American tribes created "saunas" by building dome-shaped structures that were covered in skins. A small hole was dug in the sauna floor, and red-hot rocks were placed within the hole, usually by a holy man, after which water was sprinkled on the rocks.

These saunas, or sweat lodges, were not solely used for the purpose of "sweating;" they were a means of spiritual purification, of cleansing from the inside out, and they were used before many major religious ceremonies.

As a boy I had built several sweat lodges, my best being inside a large, hollowed-out oak tree. While paddling, I began planning the design of the structure.

On either bank of the river, the damage from the storm was evident. One month prior, Scott and I had reroofed Doc's cabin, and I wondered how the new roof had survived the storm. Yet the more I thought about it, the less I worried; after all, the cabin's original roof had survived undamaged for twenty years. Once again, however, the North proved me wrong for I discovered that the roof, although still intact, was not left unimpaired. Its surface was covered with holes the size of large marbles; one hole was the size of an egg. Every day is a new day, each with its own surprises.

I entered the tool shed and grabbed an ax, a hatchet, hammer and nails, a file, and a bow saw. Because the sun was only an hour old, I came and went as quietly as I possibly could. In the "back yard," our large dome tent was set up and I could hear Scott's muffled snore through the tent's nylon walls. Soon, I was back on the river.

The trees that grew near my campsite were very large in comparison to other trees in the area. How was I, one man, going to chop any of them down, section them, bring them to the river bank, and drag them up the hill to the site I had selected. I wanted Scott to help me, yet I wanted more than anything to surprise him with a completed project. I decided to cross that bridge when I arrived back at the campsite.

As I pulled the canoe onto the riverbank, I looked up the small hill in the direction of the site. This was indeed the place. Without further delay, I picked up the ax and the bow saw and headed up the bubbling feeder stream. After a great deal of difficulty, I managed to cut down four large trees. Once they were down, I cut them into equal lengths and wrestled them into the feeder stream. From there (with some guidance from me), the logs floated down the feeder stream and into the river, where I caught them and dragged them onto the shore. I'm sure this sounds rather simple, but I can assure you it was not. I spent a lot of time getting the logs to drift down the feeder stream, not to mention the time it took to chop the trees down and cut them into sections. On one occasion, the largest log (one I ended up calling The Bastard) escaped my grasp on the riverbank, and began floating downstream. I jumped in after it, wrapped a rope around it, and dragged it back upstream.

Four hours and several blisters later, I had six logs laying in a neat row along the bank of the river. Four of these six were very large, and because the structure would not be set on footings, these were to be my foundation logs. My arms were scratched and bloody, my hands were gnarled, and my hair was knotted with tree sap, and the hardest part was yet to come . . . the hill.

For a long time I sat on top of the logs panting like a dog on a hot summer day. I sat staring up at the tiny hill before me, hoping that if I stared long enough the logs might move themselves. But behind all good things is a great deal of hard work, so without delay I grabbed one of the logs and started to work.

I began by laying the logs parallel to the river bank. To move them, I would swing each end one at a time, driving a stake into the ground to prevent the end that wasn't being swung from rolling back down the hill. The work was slow and extremely laborious. However, it was simple and honest work and I thoroughly enjoyed every minute of it. By mid-afternoon, all six logs were on top of the hill. I carefully surveyed the site trying to decide on the perfect location for the first log and also trying to decide which direction it should face.

Finally, I chose the largest of the six logs and began to drag it to its resting place. It was then that a rather strange thing happened. When the log was near the chosen spot, it seemed to roll the last half turn by itself. The log simply fit itself into place as if it had been meant to be there.

I stood back and observed the log, and for the first time I realized just how big it was. I decided this structure would be much too large for a sweat lodge. It would take far too long and far too many hot rocks to fill with steam. Now what?

With swollen fingers I brushed the lingering mosquitoes from my forehead. My eyes squinted from salty sweat, so I strolled down to the river to ponder my predicament and wash my face.

Doc's cabin was in desperate need of a cache. If his cabin caught fire, we had no emergency back-up supplies. And so, within five minutes, the structure went from being a sweat lodge to a cache. I plunged my head into the cold water, allowing it to run over my neck. Most caches are built high above the ground, safe from animals; this one was staying right where it was. If an animal really wanted to break in, he'd figure out a way, be the cache on the ground or one hundred feet above the ground.

I moved the second log into place, chuckling to myself, for the only experience I'd had building a log structure prior to this was playing with Lincoln Logs as a boy. After the second log was in place, it came time for me to cut the notches. Technically, one is supposed to use a compass to match the notch with the log upon which it will be resting. This is done by figuring out the diameter of the bottom log and scribing an arc on the top log. The arc is the section to be notched, thus providing a perfect fit. I used a more primitive fashion for cutting notches, the "Mmm yeah, that looks about right" technique. Not nearly as accurate but equally effective. After that, I picked up the ax and the notching began. I used a hatchet for the detail and touch-up work, and soon, the first notch was cut.

Before nightfall, I had the first four logs in place. I placed sphagnum moss beneath each notch to prevent the wind from coming through the cracks before the logs were finally nailed to each other. Exhausted, bloodied and blistered, I tunneled into my tent for a good night's sleep. Although my body felt as though it had been flogged, my spirit was tremendous, buoyed by the day's accomplishments, and sleep came quite easily.

The following morning I awoke with a start. I was excited and anxious to resume the construction of the new storage cache. However, as I rose from my sleeping bag, I discovered my body was not nearly as ready to work as my mind. Pain lingered from the previous day's work; I felt as though I couldn't lift my arms, let alone a log that weighed several hundred pounds.

I decided to forget about surprising Scott with the cache and decided to enlist his help in its creation instead. I realized that if I were to attempt this alone it would take three months to build and four months to recover from the hernia. Scott and I were partners, and in the long run Scott's help and advice proved more than useful. This project, like the entire northern adventure, required teamwork.

Feeling a sense of relief from not having to abuse myself any further, I hopped in the canoe and paddled toward the cabin. I could not wait to tell Scott what I had begun to build, and I could not wait for the two of us to begin working on the project together.

When I arrived at the cabin, I found Scott had just completed a new table which rested near the east wall beneath the window. We talked about the storm and I learned that I was not the only one who had been in a tent that night. I told Scott about my campsite, complimented him on the new table, and convinced him to come upstream and camp with me because I was already bored with my own company. I did not tell him about the cache; I wanted that to be a surprise. However, I'm sure Scott could tell I was up to something. On the way out, I grabbed the chain saw and more nails. Obviously, the chain saw could not be concealed, so I told Scott that we could use it to cut some firewood.

We paddled as one, silently and solemnly beyond the bivouac, and then we were within view of the first two logs in the north wall of the cache. Because he was paddling, Scott did not notice the structure. I sat in the stern of the canoe and smiled. I knew the moment he saw it, he would be more than anxious to join in the hard work. Plus, this was yet another thing we could do to impress the unimpressible Doc Forgey. Before we reached the shoreline, Scott spotted the horizontally stacked logs. "I knew you were up to something!" he shouted. "The day after the storm I noticed the ax and some other things missing from the tool shed, and right then I knew you had something up your sleeve. Yet I would have never thought you were beginning another cabin! This'll blow Forgey's mind!"

"Actually," I said, "It's a cache."

"That's one big cache. Besides, if Doc's cabin burns down, what good is a cache of food and gear without adequate shelter? Why not make an emergency 'back-up' cabin?" Scott suggested.

Scott had an excellent idea. I was surprised that I hadn't thought of building a cabin earlier. I suppose the task simply sounded too extreme, but Scott was right. Without having even picked up an ax, Scott had proved beneficial.

I took Scott on a quick tour of the area and showed him where I had cut the first few logs, describing how I had wrestled them into the feeder stream, down to the river, and finally up to the top of the hill. Scott suggested that we cut the rest of the logs further away from the cabin site. I agreed.

Soon, we were scouting along the river by canoe, checking its banks for a possible cutting site. We found the perfect spot a half mile up from our new cabin. The trees were large, straight, and growing right on the river. We decided that I would be in charge of the chain saw, thus enabling me to know the tool through and through, and decreasing the risk of injury.

Before we left the cabin site, we had measured the logs already cut with a length of rope. This would serve as our guide in cutting the other logs. Prior to cutting, we cleared the dead limbs around a tree's trunk. Two logs could be obtained from most of the trees we'd selected, and those which could not be used as timbers would serve as firewood.

Once several large trees were selected, the cutting began. The screaming of the chain saw was deafening to our ears, which were by now accustomed to near silence. Within minutes, my wool pants were covered in wood chips and sawdust. The day slowly grew hotter and the work became more intense and demanding. By late afternoon, we had cut several trees into equal lengths and had them neatly piled on the forest floor. Now we simply had to get them into the river. To say the least, "simply" was the wrong word. Even though we were only fifty yards from the shore, we nearly died hauling the logs from treeline to shoreline. The easiest way for us to move the logs was to pick up one end and "flip-flop" it to the riverbank. Finally, after many shouts, yells, and "one-two-three-heaves," the once-neat pile of logs in the woods was a neat pile of logs in the water, all lashed together. Now, all we had to do was float them downstream one half mile and haul them up the hill to the cabin site.

We could have lined them to the site (using the same technique as tracking, only guiding the object downstream) but both Scott and I were far too tired for such a task. Instead, we tethered the logs to the stern of the canoe and drifted back with them. Because of the extra drag, steering was nearly impossible, and we had no alternative but to move at the same speed as the current. After a while, we made it to shore with little difficulty. As before, the hard part was yet to come . . . dragging the logs up the hill.

We dragged the logs onto the bank, sat on the pile gazing up the tiny knoll knowing that the job would be nothing short of hell.

"Well," Scott said as he slowly stood, "This job won't get done with us just sittin' here!" He pulled his leather gloves on and wiped the sweat from his forehead with his bandanna .

I stood up slowly. "Why do today what you can put off till tomorrow?" I asked. Scott managed a laugh and we both began working, yet with less vigor. The mere thought of work seemed to rob us of strength.

Once again, we had to "flip-flop" the logs until one end (preferably the fat end) rested near the top of the hill. After that job was complete, we would grab the lower end of the log and swing it up until it was parallel to the top of the hill. Sometimes, after the log had been flip-flopped, one of us would stand at the top, the other at the bottom, and with the log between our feet, we would lift and slide it up the tiny hill foot by foot. We called this technique "caterpillaring."

By nightfall, we had six logs up the hill, with three remaining at the bottom. Our wrists bled and our backs ached; our legs and chests were scraped and scratched; and our hands were stiff and marred. However, never before had work felt so wonderful, and so rewarding.

Scott began preparing dinner, and I went down to the river to fetch some water. Then we both sat and stared at the flame glowing in the Coleman stove. Under normal circumstances, we would have built a campfire, but because of our exhaustion, we settled for the stove. As we rapidly shoveled the food into our faces, Scott and I complimented each other on the day's progress. We also talked excitedly about notching logs and building walls when the sun came up.

After dinner, we reclined against the first few logs of our cabin and peered into the river valley below. Neither of us spoke on occasions such as these. With all that rested before us, there was no need. From the west came the sound of the feeder stream, whispering faintly through the trees. Directly in front of us (to the north) rolled the river, which had aided us tremendously in our work. Below us was a cushion of spongy moss, behind us sat the fruits of our labor, and above us the starlit night expanded over the endless miles of a serene wilderness.

As the night grew old, the sky became alive with northern lights. A dancing highway of green, red, yellow and white stretched above the barren land. Their reflection could be seen in the river, and their presence could be felt in the soul. For years, this awesome spectacle has mystified, frightened, amazed and left breathless many northern woodsmen. Be they Indians, trappers, voyageurs, or explorers, the lights have made them stop dead in their tracks and gaze into the heavens. They seem to have a presence, these dancing lights, a presence that puts man in perspective upon the face of such a vast wilderness. It's something that can be felt when stepping out from a cabin door. One need not look up, for the dancing lights seem to hush the entire wilderness, and the moment the cabin door closes, neither man nor beast stirs, for it is understood that the lights are out. Often I have heard people explain in scientific terms the "hows" and "whys" of the northern lights, yet for myself, I choose not to know. Man spends too much time categorizing and too little time appreciating, rendering the valuable invisible.

Filled with a good meal, tired from the day's work, and content with the magnificent evening, Scott and I ambled off to the confines of our tent. Once inside candles were lit and, although exhausted, we could not resist talking further about the day's progress. We sketched in our journals pictures of what we thought the cabin would look like. We discussed the next location for cutting trees, and we laughed at the fact that we felt like we'd been through a war.

Never in my life have I had a "job" that was so physically demanding, and never before have I loved a job so dearly. For the next few weeks, we would awaken with the sun, and we would be disappointed when the sun set, for we could no longer work. We were far too busy to stop and consider anything along the lines of a lunch or a coffee break, whereas with my occupations in the "civilized world," these were the highlights of the day. We also learned the immense value of work. We understood that whatever we left behind was to be our legacy. In listening to music, I can understand the musician, in looking at a painting, I can see the artist. A musician can not hide himself within his song, and an artist can not hide himself within his painting; they are an intrinsic part of their art. The cabin was our song, our painting. Chances are it would far outlast Scott and me, therefore the structure had to be built to nothing less than the highest standards.

With each passing sunset, the walls of our cabin grew. Soon, we could not see over its walls, and our excitement grew as rapidly as the cabin itself.

A great deal had happened during the course of the cabin's construction. On September 4, Scott and I killed the moose, which resulted in five days of rigorous labor. We spent the greater part of three days simply butchering and packaging meat, stretching and salting the hide, and protecting the meat that wasn't being packaged from hungry martins. Any meat that wasn't packaged was thinly sliced and placed on a large smoking rack that Scott and I had built. The smoking process alone took three days and a smoky fire had to be maintained day and night.

Before the meat was taken from the rack on September 10, Doc flew in to re-supply us, yet, as always, he brought a few surprises with him. It was mid-afternoon when Scott and I heard the bush plane. We were both up in the loft, reading. The plane drew nearer, and Scott and I looked at each other over the tops of our books, then blasted out the cabin's front door. At that moment, a Cessna 185 buzzed low over the roof of the cabin, with a canoe strapped to its pontoon. Two passengers waved from the window of the small plane, and I could tell one of them was my father.

After several months alone in the bush, the arrival of visitors is a welcome occasion. It is also an exciting and frightening time for both parties, for neither knows how the other is doing. No one knew whether we were dead or alive, and vice versa.

The plane circled, tipped its wings and headed toward Landing Lake. From where we stood, we could hear the drone of the engine decrease and finally cut.

Because the cabin was in shambles, Scott and I quickly began cleaning. In only two short hours we would have visitors, one of which would be my father. He had mentioned coming in, and there had also been some talk about all of us canoeing out to Churchill.

When we had come home for Scott's skin graft I had explained to my father how I wished he could come up for a visit. Soon, he would be a visitor in our home; he would see the things that I so desperately had attempted to explain; he would witness, first-hand, the beauty and power of the North. Even though he and the rest of my family had supported my rustic northern adventure, they could never fully begin to understand or relate to the actual experience. Now, at last, I could share a small part of that adventure with someone in my family.

One can try to explain a particular experience, but until the listener has been there, he or she will never fully understand its true meaning. The map is not the country, and although it sounds foolish, some people are actually deceived by this fact. A map can show the topographics and the layout of the land, but tiny slash marks don't convey the power and velocity of the rivers they are portraying; small symbols representing muskegs don't tell how arduous travel will be through that particular wetland; nor do they tell how bad the bugs will be. A map cannot show how deep or shallow the river water will be, or where the fish congregate. A map cannot tell when the rain will come, nor can it demonstrate the bitterness of 40° below temperatures. And above all, a map cannot depict the country's beauty. All of these things cannot be explained through pictures, maps, stories, or symbols. To fully understand them, they must be experienced first-hand!

Two hours had gone by since the plane had buzzed our cabin. We'd made two batches of Kool-Aid, for we knew our visitors would be dehydrated, popped a stuff sack full of popcorn and set out a loaf of bread that Scott had prepared the previous day. A large fire was burning in the fire ring, and logs were placed around it to serve as seats. All that was left to do now was wait.

Finally, after three-and-a-half hours, we heard a faint whistle. Scott and I looked at each other, not really knowing how to react. Of course we were excited, but it was a bit odd to know that other human beings were in the area. Scott draped his capote over his shoulders, I laced up my mukluks and off we walked into the woods to find our guests.

We spotted them shortly, walking downstream toward the cabin, and I suppose I'll never be happier.

Scott said it best when we made our first swamp crossing together, "I no longer believe that hell is fire and brimstone . . . I now believe that hell is traveling through a muskeg with an over-loaded pack." From the look on my father's face, I found great truth in Scott's statement.

I grabbed his pack, gave him a hug and for a long time the two of us simply stared at each other. We were both at a loss for words, yet nothing really needed to be said. We just continued to smile and stare. I knew that my appearance must have seemed rather extraordinary to him. He wasn't used to seeing his son with a ponytail and a full beard. In spite of that, I could see in his eyes a great deal of happiness. I could see that he was truly proud of me. I put his pack on my back, put my arm around his shoulder, and began walking toward the cabin.

My father was quick to tell me that everyone back home was fine, and at the moment that was the only thing about which I was concerned.

My father and Doc had brought other guests along. There were six of us altogether at the cabin: Mark Wagstaff, executive director of the Wilderness Education Association, and Keith Tutt, a contractor from Regina, Saskatchewan were also on the plane. Although not used to the company, Scott and I enjoyed it greatly.

With tremendous pride we flaunted our moose hide as well as his broad spreading antlers. We also displayed our rack of smoked moose meat and our newly built refrigerator full of moose steaks. This seemed to impress Doc the most, for no one on past trips had ever shot a moose.

On the fourth day of our visit, we decided to canoe upstream so that everyone could see the grandest surprise of all . . . the cabin. However, first we had to stop at the bivouac site.

My father had only seen pictures of this monumental place and now he actually stood in front of what could have been the grave of one of his children. I could tell as he slowly approached that the site of the bivouac had as great an impact on him as it did on Scott and myself.

We spent a great deal of time there relating the story of that tremendous first night, then we traveled upstream for the great surprise.

Scott and I had been waiting since the start of the cabin project to show it off. That time finally was at hand. Soon, our crew was approaching the tiny knoll upon which the cabin was nestled, and even though the structure was not complete, it certainly surprised our guests.

Doc was especially appreciative, for he knew how much work was required to build a log cabin. He paced, he touched, he stared, he shook his head, and said, "I am impressed!" We knew then that we had done an exceptional job.

Because we were short on building materials such as plexi-glass, fiber-glass, wood, hinges and nails, we decided to paddle to Churchill for more supplies. Our guests had originally planned to canoe out to Churchill, saving them the cost of chartering another bush plane; therefore, it was decided that we would canoe out with them. Several days later, the six of us departed for civilization, which for Scott and me would be an adventure of a different sort.

When our four visitors had flown into the cabin, Mark was slightly ill. It just so happened that when he recovered, my father became ill (this was the day of our departure). For the next two days, while we were on the river, he was extremely sick, and Doc busied himself administering antibiotics. Finally, I caught the "sickness" and thought, without question, that I too, was going to die. It was on this day that we met our neighbors.

Because I was rendered useless, I paddled with Keith Tutt, the strongest canoeist of our group. Keith is short and built like a grizzly bear. Next to Scott, he is the first person I would pick as a canoe partner, and the last person I would want to tangle with. On this particular day, Keith was sitting in the bow of our canoe, and not only did he power the boat from the bow, he steered it as well. I don't suppose I will ever again paddle with such a strong and skilled canoeist.

As we were being tossed about on the mighty Churchill River, I heard Keith mumble something about a tent cabin. A few minutes later, he claimed that he saw smoke coming from the cabin's smoke stack. I didn't stir, I simply reclined in the back of the canoe, spinning from the painkillers that kept me alive. When Keith finally mentioned that he saw people, I sat up as attentively as I could and opened my eyes to make certain he wasn't imagining things. What he saw was no mirage, and hurriedly our three canoes were aimed for the riverbank, where our new neighbors stood.

Ernie, Robert, and Manford were all Churchill residents. They used the tent cabin, which was about 60 miles from Doc's cabin, a few times a year for hunting and fishing.

We were apprehensive at first, and so too were they, until Ernie broke the ice by saying in his Canadian accent, "You fellas look like you could use either a hot cup a' coffee, or a cold beer . . . Aye?" From then on, they treated us with tremendous northern hospitality.

After spending several days with the three moose hunters, we arrived in Churchill. Because it's a one-horse town, with a population of 700, it did not produce near the culture shock that Chicago had when we'd first left for Scott's skin graft. For the first time in months, we were able to enjoy a drink and shoot a game of pool with the locals. Funny how the little things become so important. We also talked to friends and family back home, which was a bitter-sweet experience.

Because we could not find all our building materials in Churchill, Scott and I planned to take the day-and-a-half train ride south to Thompson. Before we departed, we went to the airport to say farewell to my dad and the gang.

I suppose that both my father and I welled-up a bit, yet after a hug, he shook my hand and told me how proud he was, and how supportive my mother and the rest of our family was. This to me was all important. I smiled and waved as he walked slowly through his gate, and said, "See ya next year."

September 25, 1991:

Once again the bush plane's propeller chopped through the northern sky. Scott and I remained silent, watching once more the plane's shadow dance swiftly over the endless miles of muskeg.

Soon, we were helping our pilot tether the plane to the shoreline of the river near the cabin. After all our gear was unloaded, he said he had to leave.

"Well, why don't you come up and see the cabin?" we asked. "Yeah, would ya like a cup of coffee? After all, you don't have to leave right now!"

He was our last link to "civilization," and we knew he would be the last person we would see for three months.

Finally, after showing the cabin, we waved good-bye and watched him tip the plane's wings as he faded into a tiny speck on the vast horizon. All was silent, and solitude shrouded the country. The colors of fall were much more prominent, and the cool air made us turn up our collars against the cold.

The cabin seemed somewhat sad in the absence of our visitors' smiling faces, so Scott and I commenced cleaning again. This, for some reason, always took our minds away from negativity.

Still, for the next week, Scott and I were depressed. Going back into the cabin experience is as much of a culture shock as coming out, and during that week this fact was evident. It wasn't so much that we missed civilization, but it had been difficult to talk to loved ones back home during our brief foray into Churchill and to tell them that we would not see them for three more months.

We also realized that soon winter would be upon us and with winter came darkness, silence, and cold. Eighteen hours of darkness would urge us to stay inside. What was once a singing wilderness would become a sleeping wilderness. And even though the river would still sing, its song would be muted by three feet of ice.

Seven days later I awakened to see the ground covered with snow. Two miles upstream a cabin waited patiently for completion, and because Doc had paid for all of the building supplies, we felt obligated to finish what we'd started. With new found energy, I jumped downstairs and started cooking a large breakfast.

Soon Scott awakened and cursed the blanket of white. He wasn't depressed to see snow, but he knew we had a great deal of work left unfinished.

When he came down from the loft, I handed him a cup of coffee and we agreed to head upstream and finish the cabin. Quite frankly, we wanted to get out of Doc's cabin. So much was changing in that wild land, and we were two spectators standing on the sideline of self-pity rather than participating in the game.

After breakfast we loaded the canoe, pointed the bow upstream, and headed for our new cabin. As we paddled the feeling of adventure returned, along with the need for physical labor; once again we were alive.

Work that day was rigorous. We chopped down several more trees and did not stop until all of the logs rested atop the tiny hill. The weather was cold and the morning's gentle snow was replaced by sleet. In spite of that, Scott and I continued our work.

Finally, when darkness began to fall, we prepared a quick freeze-dried meal and dragged ourselves into the tent, too exhausted for anything but sleep.

Throughout the course of the next two weeks, something strange happened. We were expecting sleet and snow for the work days ahead because late September is typically synonymous with "freeze-up." Yet, amazingly, the skies cleared and the weather was beautiful. Each day we waited for some sort of drastic change in the temperature, but nothing happened. The mornings and nights were freezing, but the days were classic examples of Indian summer.

As the days became shorter the wall logs slowly crept inward to form the roof. It was like watching a film in slow motion. Soon, we were building frames to fit our pre-cut plexiglass windows, and after the windows were constructed, we cut holes in the cabin walls to match. What once had looked like a box of logs was now beginning to look like a cabin of logs, each fitted together with pride and care.

Each night, while in the tent, we tried to guess which would be the first night we'd be able to stay in the cabin.

We cut small saplings to serve as roof rafters, over which we would lay heavy plastic and tar paper. We "borrowed" the small wood stove that was sitting in the south wing of Doc's cabin. It would have to suffice, for we had nothing else. Also in the south wing was the stove-pipe's thimble (a small piece of asbestos placed between the wall and the stove-pipe to prevent the wall from burning), which we "borrowed" as well.

The most difficult thing about building the log cabin was cutting holes in its walls to serve as windows, doors and stove-pipe exits. We had cut down the trees, cleared the limbs, sectioned the logs, floated them down the river, dragged them up on the shore, flip-flopped them up the hill, notched them, stacked them, and tacked them. That's a lot of work, so you can understand why it was hard for us to stab these walls with the nose of a screaming, oil spitting, chain saw.

However, it had to be done, and every hole was fitted snugly with a window, a door, or a stove-pipe.

By the first week in October we had the roof on, the stove rigged, and three of the four windows in place. Technically, all that was left was to cut the fourth window, build a front door, and construct a table and two bunks inside.

The building of the front door and the cabin's furniture went smoothly. However, in our haste for the perfect cabin, we ran into a slight problem with the window. On the north wall, (the wall facing the river), we had planned to install two vertical windows side by side with approximately two feet between them. We cut the first window, making certain that it was perfectly straight. Because these windows were on the north wall, they had to be perfect. It wasn't that we didn't care about the rest of the cabin, but the north wall was most noticeable, and we had used only our best logs in its construction.

The first window looked great, but while admiring it, Scott observed, "Perhaps this is a stupid question, but if we place an identical window next to this one, what will support the logs that make up that two feet of space between the windows?"

Before the question reached my ears, I realized what he was saying. For the next 45 minutes, we stared stupidly at our ridiculous blunder. I couldn't believe that in our haste, we had never stopped to consider that one detail. It wasn't so much that we were rushing simply to get done; we were excited about what we called the D.O.C. (day of completion). In our haste we had become a bit careless.

We continued to stare, attempting to somehow solve the puzzle. We thought of leaving in only one window and forgetting about the second altogether, yet that would make the cabin look off balance. We thought of somehow turning the one window into a large window, yet that would weaken our beautiful north wall, as well as make it look tacky.

Finally, we decided to cut a second window regardless of the outcome. Before beginning, we nailed two strong saplings on either side of the wall to serve as supports. The cutting began. Both Scott and I held our breath as the chain saw screamed, chewed, spit and sputtered through the beautiful wall. After several minutes the logs that needed to fall out for the window fell and the others remained intact.

In a total of nineteen working days, the two of us had built the most beautiful cabin in the North, and we stared at it as though we were gazing at the Northern Lights. We agreed that this was, by far, the greatest accomplishment of our lives. We had started with nothing more than a "will to do," and we had used nothing more than simple tools, our hands, and our minds.

We walked around the cabin time and time again,

commenting on certain logs, for each had a story to tell. The one above the door (even though it does not rest on the north wall) is the most beautiful, the second log up on the west wall is The Bastard, but we called it that only out of respect, for it had sapped a great deal of our strength. The logs on the north wall are the straightest, and second log up on the east wall is the most aged and has the most character.

For the remainder of the day, we cleaned the front and back yards and finished the cabin's interior. Never had I been so satisfied with myself, never had I been so happy. And as we finished our fine-tuning, I took tremendous pride in the fact that this would indeed be our legacy. Stories of our cabin would appear in the journals of other adventures, for this, without question, was the best damn cabin in the North.

The date was October 10, 1991; neither Scott nor I could sit still because it was to be the first night we would spend in our new cabin. While in Thompson, we had purchased a bottle of Hudson Bay scotch, to be used solely for the purpose of christening the completed cabin. After starting a small blaze in our stove, we prepared a freeze-dried meal, bannock (unleavened bread), and popcorn (our usual meal during the cabin-building project). With dinner quickly down the hatch, I took out our favorite tin cups, and poured a drink to toast our accomplishment.

One toast led to another and another, and soon we noticed a strong odor of smoke lurking in the tiny room. Of course, it's only natural for a cabin with a wood stove to smell like smoke, yet the odor was getting heavy and I noticed my stomach feeling . . . well . . . quite queasy, a queasy that was not brought about by the alcohol.

In our medical kit we carried a small carbon monoxide tester and we decided to break its seal to see if that might be the problem. Moments after the plastic was removed, the C.M. tester turned black. Its color could not have been painted any darker with a felt-tipped marker; we were definitely at risk.

Quickly, we plunged out of the cabin, drinking in the fresh air and walked over to the north wall where the stove-pipe protruded. Nine times out of ten the wind in this country blows from the north, and even though we had a "T"-section at the end of our stove-pipe, the wind was still forcing the smoke back through the pipe and into the cabin.

We corrected the problem by installing a 90-degree elbow in the pipe, making it perpendicular, rather than parallel, to the ground. Both Scott and I are still alive, so the improved pipe worked well enough, but we were a bit apprehensive about falling asleep in the cabin that night.

When we awakened the following morning, there was snow on the ground, and from that day forth we weren't to see the brown earth again. The weather had opened a door for us to work and the door had remained open just long enough for us to complete our cabin-building tasks.

On December 24, 1991, Doc flew into the cabin for our final days in the North Country. On Christmas Day, we all walked upstream to show him the cabin. He was beside himself when he saw how beautiful it was, and once inside, we told Doc that, because he had helped us finance our expedition, the cabin was his Christmas present. He told us later that it was the greatest present he'd ever received!

We Built Ourselves A Cabin

We built ourselves a cabin, yet to some a simple shack; and we built it when we were much younger lads. The walls were made of solid spruce, the roof was tamarack; and it fulfilled the tameless dreams we've always had.

We wrestled with the Norland, a trusty axe that was our friend; and we downed the logs ourselves at cutting site. Then down the stream we'd float them, and we'd fit them end to end, and its walls they seemed to grow with every night.

Until at last she was complete, Oh how we loved her so; as we stared at her from all the angled sights. We spent the night within her arms, and peered out of our window, and behold we gazed on gallant Northern Lights.

Cloaked in colored splendor, they were gleaming there above us and we simply had no humble words to say. For they shimmered with approval, 'twas an omen there before us and with open arms they welcomed us to stay.

I have wintered in her since then, while the freezing breezes dance; yet warm our cabin sits within the grove. And while I sip away my coffee, I am somewhat in a trance by a soothing song that sings within its stove.

Yet her windows they are cracked now, and her singing stove is silent, and her roof it sags quite sadly with the snows. Yet she's stood in arid sunlight and survived the storms so violent, yes she's wrestled with the season's changing blows.

And I am growing older, see my legs they shake and shiver, but our cabin is still standin' on the hill.
Within the pillowed pine boughs, oh it's nestled by the river, I shall leave her to the children in my will.

In hopes that they will listen to the voice the woods will give, and hear their names within the wind that calls.
With hearts untamed and souls unmaimed, from man they'll freely live, to find themselves within those cabin walls.

Scott struggles to pull his supply sled over the frozen
waves of First Falls. This trip was one of many we took
away from the cabin.

Cabin Fever

Call it whatever you wish. Bunk-bound, snow-stuck, log-locked, or bush-wacky, if you've ever spent a significant amount of time in the backcountry, then you can relate to cabin fever. If perhaps you are not yet familiar with this sickness, allow me to explain its symptoms.

Cabin fever usually strikes in the winter months, when darkness prevails and plummeting temperatures restrict outdoor activities. It usually hits when the snow is piled high and it always begins with boredom.

This isn't your average "nothin' to do" boredom, but serious "pre-depression" boredom. One day you awaken to discover that nothing sounds appealing. Your beautiful surroundings suddenly look dull, the thought of chopping wood or doing any other form of work makes your stomach turn, and the thought of reading another book makes you want to scream. You feel no desire to carry on a conversation with your partner, for you've each heard the same old stories a million times, and you would give your left arm to do something as simple as watch an old television show.

Once the boredom boils in your blood for a while, the next phase of cabin fever slowly sets in . . . depression. You get a serious case of the blues, and a serious case of homesickness. You start to think about friends and family back home and how they are so rapidly getting on with their lives while you sit in a log cabin secluded from everything.

Finally, once you've become really blue, you enter a state of self-pity. You somehow feel as though you may be missing out on all kinds of wonderful things happening in the "civilized world," and you begin to believe that all of the people who deemed you crazy when you embarked on your adventure just may have been right.

As I mentioned earlier, Scott and I both received extensive medical training from Dr. Forgey before coming north. However, he had failed to offer us a cure for this most common northern illness.

It was during difficult times such as these that Scott and I would do the only logical thing we could, and that was to go camping. These "escapes" were essential to our sanity. Getting out and away from the cabin was not only healthy, but necessary as well. We managed to take several trips away from home that winter and cabin fever was not our only reason for leaving.

One of the great things about our very first week in the frozen Canadian wilderness was that it had eliminated our fears of cold-weather camping. Our bivouac, and all that had come with it, had forced us to create an efficient winter camping system and although our technique didn't "go by the book," it worked best for us. Oddly enough, most of our adventures away from the cabin occurred in the dead of winter (no pun intended) when the weather was at its worst.

On November 12, 1991, a month after we had finished our log cabin, Scott pulled out our weathered, coffee-stained map and, after giving it some review, said, "Let's load up the sleds, strap on the skis, lock the place up and head upstream to South Fork."

Since Doc built his cabin, nearly twenty years ago, we had never heard of anyone who had traveled more than ten miles upstream and South Fork was nearly thirty miles away. I glanced casually outside to where our thermometer sat perched on the cabin's window sill . . . 32° below zero. After downing the remaining coffee, I smiled and asked, "When do we leave?" The rest of the morning was spent drinking more coffee and neatly organizing food and supplies into two large duffels.

Food consisted of freeze-dried meals, a small amount of oil and breading mix for frying wild game (if we were lucky enough to get anything), powdered drink mix, instant pudding for dessert, bannock, instant potatoes (one of our favorites), and, although we preferred to make our own, instant gravy. We also brought a lot of coffee, but that goes without saying.

As far as equipment, we brought the basics. Our faithful tent, along with our faithful stove, a small board that served as a table for the stove, as well as a cutting board, sleeping bags, fuel, a change of warm clothing, matches, a condensed version of our medical kit, toiletries, journals and a small travel game. We also brought along a couple of flares, the coffee-stained map and Betsie, a twelve-gauge shotgun borrowed from a friend prior to our departure. (Did I mention a lot of coffee?)

Just two hours after Scott's announcement, we were bolting the cabin's front door, strapping on our skis, and preparing to disconnect ourselves from the security of our cabin.

Skiing upriver was not a very difficult task and with each bend our excitement mounted. We were gliding through un-trodden country, and even though we didn't know where we were going, we couldn't wait to get there.

The sleds slid easily behind us in the powdery snow, and it felt good to be exploring. It's an experience that brings the kid out of anyone, and we were no exception.

We glided through never-ending crystal waves of snow, watching the pristine scenery drift by, until we reached First Falls, the first set of rapids upstream from the cabin. Because its waters were so fierce, it had not yet frozen. By our calculations, we were about seven miles from the cabin. Not too bad for our first day out.

Scott and I quickly found the perfect site to set up camp. The sun was beginning to dip below the horizon, spinning long gray shadows in the woods and we hastily went about pitching the tent and gathering snow for water. The temperature dropped quickly and the thought of climbing into a warm sleeping bag was more than enticing.

Moments later the tent was up and our one-burner stove was hissing away, generating enough heat to keep us warm. Every now and then, Scott would open the tent door to gather snow for water, and when the hot and cold air clashed, a huge billow of steam would rise and freeze on the tent roof.

Dinner was, as always on the trail, washed down with hot tea. We were so exhausted that conversation drifted idly from subject to subject. There we sat . . . burrowed in our bags, miles from the cabin, hundreds of miles from other humans, in 30° below temperatures, discussing everything from politics to Plato, from religion to rebellion, from girlfriends to grandparents. No one in the world knew where we were. We didn't even know exactly where we were, for that matter, and quite frankly we didn't care. We were living an adventure within an adventure, and other than our well-being, we cared about little else.

Outside the wind worked diligently, changing the many patterns of snow on the river. I pictured the animals of the forest curled up in the snow, content with surviving yet another day in the frozen North. Somewhere an owl whoo-whooed, and after burrowing more deeply into my bag, I fell asleep.

The bony hands of the cold shook me awake the following morning and I cursed its rudeness while I fumbled with the stove. Its tank had run dry the night before leaving me with the tedious task of attempting to pour super-cooled fuel into a half-inch diameter hole. The aluminum bottle in which the fuel was stored was much like a container of liquid nitrogen and my bare hand stuck to its frosted surface. With great care and patience, I managed to fill and ignite the stove.

Because Scott and I had spent the past two months living in the cabin we had become rather spoiled, forgetting what cold-weather camping entailed. However, after a hot cup of coffee and some freeze-dried hash browns, we were back in the game, and ready to hit the trail.

As we drew nearer to First Falls, the sound of the roaring water grew louder, and Scott and I soon realized that we would have to hike up into the woods, away from the river, to avoid the rushing water.

Skiing through the dense spruce trees with a sled would have been nearly impossible, so we decided to leave our skis behind and drag our sleds through the forest on foot first. As soon as we were safely beyond the falls, Scott offered to return for the skis and poles.

I was sitting on my sled sipping coffee from our thermos and waiting for Scott to return when I heard a yell. Without thinking, I began to run toward the yell. The gaping hole in the ice of the river told the story well enough. Fortunately, Scott was laying on the riverbank a short distance from the hole . . . unfortunately, he was soaking wet from his waist down. Perhaps only a minute had passed since the accident had occurred, but Scott was already shaking uncontrollably from the cold.

"We have to set up the tent and we'd better do it quick!" Scott said, as he stood and began jogging to our sleds.

The temperature was at least 20º below, maybe colder, and I could hear the ice that formed on Scott's wool pants crack as he walked.

"I have a better idea than the tent," I said.

Quickly I grabbed the sled's leash and dragged the load up the hill to the hydro-station. A small structure that served as a water-monitoring station for the Little Beaver River, placed there by the Canadian government to monitor water levels. A solar panel was sitting on the roof that gave life to scientific equipment inside. This structure, about the size of two telephone booths, is the only evidence of humans anywhere near our cabin. I figured rather than waste time setting up the tent we could simply use it, along with the aid of a camp stove, as sort of an emergency warming booth.

When I reached the front of the station, my mouth fell open in amazement. Lo and behold, there was a lock on the door! This thing was as far away from vandals as it could possibly be. However, as I slid a shell into Betsie's chamber, I figured it wasn't far enough.

Ka-Boom. The shotgun rang out and the lock went flying from the door. To hell with government property, this was an emergency. I fired up the stove and placed it in the structure. We were carrying a back-up stove, which I fueled up and ignited as well. Meanwhile, Scott changed into his dry clothing and hovered over the warmth of the stoves.

The tiny structure became warm instantly with the two of us inside and both stoves roaring. I pulled the liners out of Scott's boots, only to discover that they were surprisingly dry. Scott took off his socks and began massaging his feet.

"I thought for sure I was going down!" he said solemnly. "I thought for sure I was a dead man!"

We both shook at the possibility of what could have happened, and we stood silently, drying the gear, until the fuel burned out.

The hole in the ice reminded me of how fragile life is and how quickly it can be erased. Once more we packed up our gear, loaded it onto the sleds and headed upstream, this time proceeding with greater caution.

The wind bit into our faces, numbing our noses and cheeks, yet despite the cold, we were content.

We walked for several hours, taking breaks every now and then to nibble on munchies or sip coffee from the thermos. Each time we stopped, we would unfold the map and attempt to figure out where we were. Finally, we could travel no further. Because we had lost so much time with the accident, dusk fell upon us quickly. Ahead in the distance we spotted a reasonable place to set up camp.

As we drew nearer, a scrawny red fox darted across the river toward the opposite bank, glancing back only once at the two oddly-clad trespassers. I thought about how we had to bundle up to shield ourselves from the elements, and how we had to drag two sleds loaded with supplies to keep ourselves alive, while he needed nothing but his cunning instincts.

That night we set up camp and talked about how lucky we were to be able to sit and enjoy each other's company. It could have gone either way for Scott on that ice. The lesson tempered our confidence, and travel would now be made with more caution.

I had a difficult time falling asleep that night, for I kept thinking about what I would have done had things gone the other way. How would I have told his friends and family? My thoughts went back to the fox we had seen only a few hours ago. To him and to all the creatures of this frozen land, death was merely a part of life. Insecurity was the ticket to staying alive. Finally, exhaustion got the best of me and I fell asleep.

"Zing" was the word for the day. It is a word for which Scott deserves credit. Zing was the name chosen for our particular style of coffee. We thought of others, like Manitoba mud, black magic and camp coffee, but Zing seemed to fit the bill. "Zing . . . one sip equals one cup . . . one cup equals twenty!" After several cups, we realized just how powerful it really was. Coffee was a staple for us at the cabin and it always seemed to be made with twice the punch on camp-outs.

The sun glistened on the endless sea of snow that day and the temperature warmed up a bit allowing Scott and me the freedom of fairly easy travel. After an hour or so of skiing, we came to the second set of falls upstream from the cabin (appropriately named Second Falls.)

The water washed over the ice on which we skied, so from time to time we had to clear our skis from the slush that froze to them. Also, because we were so near the bank, we had to fight our way through tangled alder and willow bushes. To add to our difficulties, a fifteen-foot wall of rock jutted out into the screaming rapids, forcing us up into the woods.

The trip around Second Falls took well over an hour, but we were rewarded afterwards, for we were now traveling in unknown territory.

After another hour or so, Scott spotted several ptarmigan resting on the rocky shore.

"Well," I said, removing the shotgun from its scabbard, "I suggest we set up camp for the night and prepare a feast of ptarmigan for dinner."

"You took the words right out of my mouth." Scott said, and with that I began walking slowly toward the small group of birds.

BOOM. The gun thundered, shattering the silence of the river valley. With three shots I killed five plump birds, (two with one shot). With a broad smile on my face, I proudly brought my trophies back to where Scott stood.

Scott set up the tent while I busied myself cleaning the birds. I encountered a problem in this task, for in order to remove the plump breasts from the birds, I first had to remove my heavy down mitts. By the time I had finished cleaning the third bird, my hands were so cold they would not function properly. Scott had since finished setting up the tent, so he came out to clean the last two birds.

Finally, we had five beautiful pieces of meat soaking in a pot of warm salted water. Scott began boiling water for tea, and I dug through the food bag, removing the instant potatoes, freeze-dried corn, oil, frying mix, instant gravy, and the instant chocolate pudding for dessert. We sliced the meat off the breast bones and placed the halves into the bag of frying mix, shaking the bag to cover each piece evenly. Scott poured us each a cup of tea, and then poured some oil into the skillet. We watched the meat turn golden brown in the frying pan, and just before the pieces were cooked to perfection, Scott added boiling water to the corn, potatoes, and gravy to hydrate them.

A rich aroma filled the tiny tent, and our stomachs growled at the sight of such a noble feast.

Before eating, all of the food was neatly arranged in our frying pan. We sprinkled the meat and the potatoes with lemon pepper and a dash of onion salt, after which we poured a thin layer of gravy over each. A small amount of butter was melted over the corn and the potatoes, and because it looked so fancy, we took pictures of the feast.

At last, we could refrain no longer, and we began filling our faces. For the next ten minutes there was silence in the tent. Our only form of communication was an occasional wide-eyed glance, followed by a rolling of the eyes. This particular meal was the best one we had eaten since we'd landed, and we were eating it miles away from the cabin in a tiny dome tent on the bank of a frozen river.

After all of the pots were licked clean, we climbed into our bags and enjoyed another cup of hot tea.

Our next day of travel brought us to the third and final set of rapids, which we ended up naming Bastard Rapids. This stretch of whitewater was mostly free of ice, boiling as it rolled toward the Churchill River. Scott and I had no choice but to move away from the river's edge, hiking over the rock cliffs and through the woods.

Every now and then, we would hike to the edge of the cliffs and peer down into the violent water. Its color was a rich bronze and it carried foam upon its back, created by the constant turbulence.

Travel at this point was at its worst. Sleds became caught in the trees, snowdrifts hindered hiking, and the rapids seemed as though they would never cease. Yet we plowed ahead, determined to reach the South Fork.

Several times along the traverse we would stop, drink some coffee and eat smoked moose meat. Darkness was beginning to descend on the frozen terrain, and Scott and I were beginning to wonder whether we would have to camp on the cliffs.

Just before we set up camp, I peered through the trees and saw a calm spot in the river. According to our map, this was the mouth of Bastard Rapids.

Although we were hungry and exhausted, we stretched the day and camped a half-mile upstream from the roaring water.

In the tent that night, we reviewed the map and found only eight miles stood between us and our goal. However, we also discovered that because of the accident at First Falls, we were running low on fuel. We had enough for three more nights out, if we were lucky, but knew by now nothing ever worked according to plan in this country.

Excitement filled the air the following morning, for it could be our day of achievement. Camp was quickly dismantled and soon we were on our way. We knew if we did not reach South Fork this day, we would have to turn back.

Scott and I skied silently and vigorously, but after several hours, we became frustrated because we were not at the fork yet. We anxiously peered around each bend in the river, hoping to discover our goal, but each bend brought only more trees, and flat terrain.

By this time, we had gone beyond the edge of the map. The sun was rapidly disappearing behind the trees, and although neither of us wanted to admit it, we knew that we had to set up camp and accept defeat with humility.

Scott loaded the sleds full of snow for water, and I pitched the tent and fired up the stove. Nothing quite compares with climbing into a warm tent at the end of a hard day's travel, sipping tea and discussing the great things that we'd seen along the way.

So we didn't make it to the fork. As far as we were concerned, the trip was a huge success. We had seen places no one in the history of the cabin had seen.

That evening, we discussed with enthusiasm all of the great things that we had accomplished while living in the North. It's one thing to stay in a secluded cabin for nearly ten months, but it's another thing to have explored the area as thoroughly as we had, to have killed a moose and to have built a cabin from scratch.

We both slept soundly that night and the following day we packed up and headed for home. We figured heading downstream would be the easy part of our adventure, but of course we were incorrect.

Ice bridges that had been safe to cross on the trip upstream had since fallen into the water forcing us into the trees more often; temperatures had been constantly rising and falling, causing the ice to buckle, and several more inches of snow had fallen. Because we were anxious to get home, the trails of the trip downstream made the journey work instead of play. Also, our fuel shortage allowed us only two more nights of warmth. We had to cover thirty-five miles in three days, which is not an easy task when skiing on a temperamental river. In spite of the obstacles, we trudged on.

On our first day of hiking downstream, our thermos fell out of the sled. Scott noticed the missing "gem," and said he had to go back for it. We covered at least three miles that day, and had no idea how far back the thermos was. Still, Scott vowed to find it.

To most people, this notion might seem somewhat absurd. Why not simply leave it behind? You must understand that items taken for granted in civilization are treated with the highest respect in cabin country. Whether it was a cooking utensil, or a six-hundred-dollar sleeping bag, there was no such thing as an easy replacement. So, Scott added two extra miles to his trip to retrieve the precious thermos.

That evening we camped on the cliffs halfway down Bastard Rapids. We had traveled nearly twelve miles that day and a majority of that travel had been bushwhacking. The temperatures were beginning to plummet, and before climbing into the tent we could hear our breath freeze, sounding much like the spray emitted from a squirt bottle. We could also hear the ice pop and crack in the frozen parts of the river.

The following day began, literally, on thin ice. Because there was a good ice shelf throughout the rest of Bastard Rapids, we decided to ski on it rather than hike through the trees. Halfway through the rapids, Scott skied down a small ice fall, and the sled that he was harnessed to began to pass him on his right side. Under normal circumstances, this would not have been a problem, but just before the sled was in his view, it began slipping into the boiling open water.

I screamed as loudly as I could over the noise of the river hoping to give Scott time to save not only his sled but his life as well. Ice makes for poor traction, especially on skis, so had the sixty-pound sled gone into the water, there would have been no escape. Scott would have been a victim of the roaring river. Luckily, he managed to pull the sled away from the leaping water.

Once more, we decided to bypass the risks of riverside travel by heading into the trees, and once again, we became coach travelers in a first-class land. Even so, we managed to cover thirteen miles that day.

By now, we were as exhausted as we could possibly be, but we were near the spot where we had camped our first night out. We had one more night's worth of fuel, and Scott and I talked eagerly about eating the remainder of our food. We also could not wait to climb into a warm tent, thaw out our ice-covered gear, sip tea and swap stories.

The moon rose in the east full and bright, and the temperature could not have been any higher than 40° below. Scott and I had to set up camp quickly to keep from getting colder.

I set up the tent and Scott gathered snow. Whether it was from the cold or the thought that I would soon be warm, my hands shook uncontrollably. My fingers seemed to turn into stone and, again, I had to watch them to complete a simple task, for nothing could be accomplished by touch alone.

At long last, the tent was up and a sled full of snow was placed at the door. I dug through the duffels and grabbed the stove. For some reason, it felt unusually light, and I couldn't remember if I had filled its tank that morning or not. Behind me, Scott was jumping up and down to keep the blood from solidifying in his veins.

I placed the stove in the snow and proceeded to look for our last fuel bottle. I still felt certain that I had filled the stove that morning. When I found the bottle I discovered that indeed I had, for it was empty.

Indian legend has it that small people, called Mimmiguesoes, live in the vast unexplored reaches of the North. They are known for their trickery and practical joking, so whenever a hole appeared in a canoe, or a paddle mysteriously vanished, the Mimmiguesoes were always to blame.

I had always enjoyed reading about these legends, but never fully believed in their existence . . . until that night!

"Scott," I said solemnly.

"What?" he replied, still bouncing and slapping his arms violently.

"We have no fuel."

As soon as the words left my mouth, Scott's bouncing ceased. In the silence of that moment, you could very easily have heard a downy snowflake hit the ground.

I squinted my eyes and hunched my shoulders, expecting to hear a string of curses shatter the star-filled sky, but instead I heard laughter. Not just a chuckle, but a full-bellied laugh. I looked over my shoulder at Scott, who was laying on his back laughing hysterically.

Although I wanted to cry, I found myself following suit. For the next five minutes we laughed, until tears froze our eyes shut. Even after gaining our composure, a mere glance at one another would send us back into hysterics.

Finally, Scott suggested we build a raging fire to brighten our spirits and that was exactly what we did. We quickly fashioned a tripod over the flames, and soon the water in our tea kettle was boiling.

Scott and I sat so close to the fire that we nearly melted our clothing, and while we guzzled hot tea Scott asked, "How in the hell did that fuel leak out of the stove anyway?"

I looked him dead in the eye and replied in all seriousness, "I bet it was the Mimmiguesoes."

Scott stared at me with a straight face for a long time and then exploded into such a fit of laughter that I thought his ribs would collapse. I, of course, did the same.

We retreated to the tent, and even though we were both nearly hypothermic, Scott continued to badger me. Each time he'd say Mimmiguesoe, he would shake his head and bust out laughing. However, as I climbed into my sleeping bag and attempted to get warm, I thought for certain I heard the echoes of high-pitched laughter from somewhere deep in the forest.

Maybe . . . just maybe . . . Naaaa!

Unfortunately, the next morning was no laughing matter. To begin with, neither Scott nor I had slept much that night. Normally, with the heat of the stove, we were allowed the luxury of packing everything in the warmth of the tent.

This particular morning, however, we had to psych ourselves up before facing the cold and packing our gear. On the count of three we jumped out of our bags, and with frozen fingers began stuffing gear into its appropriate place.

Never before have I felt such physical pain from such extreme temperatures. It seemed as though my hands were resting in a pot of boiling water, and once more we began to shake uncontrollably.

After everything was packed, we started taking down the tent, only to discover that the joints of the poles were welded with thick beads of ice. To disconnect the poles, we had to breathe heavily on the joints and force them apart.

The tent was finally folded, placed in the bottom of the sled, and once the duffels were lashed in place, Scott and I were on our way home. We only had ten miles to go before we would be sitting by a warm wood-burning stove sipping a cup of coffee.

For the first five miles, nothing was said. We skied vigorously, attempting to defeat the cold. Neither Scott nor I had anything to eat or drink that morning and because of our activity, our bodies were desperately in need of fuel. But onward we skied, hoping that around the next bend we would find familiar sights or landmarks, but everything looked the same.

The speed at which we traveled was generated by our anxiousness. Eight miles had fallen behind us, and still neither of us spoke; we continued to slide one foot in front of the other over the powdery snow.

I was nearly to the point of dropping when I finally took my eyes from the ground and looked downstream. The movement of my skis ceased; I stood in my tracks and stared. Scott, who was skiing next to me, stopped and did the same.

There it sat, amongst the gallant spruce trees, empty and black with the log shutters hanging lazily over its windows. It was our cabin, at last. The cabin that Scott and I had built with our hands, sitting silently wrapped in a coat of drifted snow.

We had never seen it from this distance and for a long time we stood in the frigid cold with broad smiles stretched upon our wind-bitten faces.

For the moment my aching muscles relaxed, and I began to think, as we slowly trudged up the slope toward the front door, what this structure symbolized for Scott and me. This was home! In spite of the fact that it was without modern conveniences and neighbors, this was our first real residence.

And yet, another home awaited us more than a thousand miles away, waiting in a fast-paced land inhabited by family and loved ones, but also by headlines and deadlines. It almost seemed like an imaginary place, since I hadn't seen it in such a long time. It seemed to be a million miles away, trapped within the pages of some melodramatic fairy tale. There, the song of the whispering pines was replaced by the sound of clicking heels and ticking clocks.

Scott un-bolted the cabin's front door and stepped inside.

"It's good to be home!" he said heartily.

I stood outside for one long bittersweet moment. The setting sun licked my face and the tree tops brushed the crimson sky. For that moment, I felt homesick for that seemingly imaginary and faraway place, yet as I looked upstream at the trail we'd just made, I felt content with where I stood.

Slowly, I closed the door behind our adventure, much like I close the pages of my journals today. And for now . . . just for now . . . I closed the door on my other home a thousand miles away as well.

"It most certainly is good to be home," I agreed . . . "Where shall we go next time?"

"Let us probe the silent places;
let us seek what luck betide us;
let us journey to a lonely land I know.
There's a whisper on the night wind;
and a star agleam to guide us,
and the wild is calling, calling let us go."

Robert Service

A Poem for My Partner

Well it looks like this is it, my friend, with the closing of the year. Our adventure is drawing to an end, but before we pack our gear; I'd like for us to just look back and see how things were then, Reminisce on life within our shack and say remember when.

Remember when we landed at the wrong end of the lake? We felt like we'd been stranded; two Cheechakos on the break.

And remember how the cold did crack the trees about our feet? And the night from hell in the ol' bivouac, how we hugged to share the heat. Oh you and I we held our breath and that's where the stories begin; for we both nearly froze to death . . . my God, remember when?

Remember when you saw your toe (well, how could you forget?) 'Twas bit to the bone in the bivouac show, ahh the evening of regret. And then we found our home to be and met our neighbor Pete. The pine squirrel that we loved to see and how he loved to eat.

Remember the games of chess that we shared with the pieces too tiny to see? Whether we won or we lost neither one really cared, just a game over coffee or tea.

Remember swimming in the stream of gold, how ol' Grundy would fill us with fear? While bulldogs went buzzing psychotically bold and they'd blast us with bites on the rear. And then we would pan in the smooth speckled sands in hope that we might strike it rich. We never got much but wrinkly hands, yet they were clean and that was a switch.

Remember the nights of the Northern Lights as we breathlessly gazed at the sky? They toiled and boiled and danced with delight as we shook with a sobering sigh.

And remember the campfires that we have shared and the dreams that we'd both talked about? Expressions accented by flickering flares till the last of the embers went out.

Remember our cabin at Paradise Creek that you and I built with our hands? Remember her stove-pipe and how it did leak, so quiet and still now she stands. 'Twas a classy old cabin and oh what a view (how 'bout the diagonal floor?) And who built that ol' cabin, damn right me and you, with the moose antlers over the door.

And the moose, the moose; how could I forget that bull with the wide spreading rack. He almost weighed a ton, I'll bet, for he damn near broke our backs.

And remember the night when we almost went mad, and how we were singin' the blues. Then the chopper came in and boy were we glad, for they brought us a bottle of booze.

And how 'bout the trip past the edge of the map, our trip of determination. And how you broke through the thin ice trap, our last hope was the hydrostation. And I blew off the lock with our trusty shotgun, for I thought that we might lose your toe.

Such adventures we've shared 'neath the midnight sun, only you and I will know. So it looks like this is it, old friend, we've shared a common strife. We're partners now until the end, and brothers now for life.

It certainly has flown by fast as those times that we've been through; the memories of our cabin past, all shared by me and you.

Well . . . just steer clear of the trodden track and if times get rough, well then, reminisce on life within our shack, smile and say

"Remember when!"